In the Kingdom of Grass

THE GREAT PLAINS PHOTOGRAPHY SERIES

Margaret A. MacKichan   Bob Ross

In the Kingdom of Grass

University of Nebraska Press   Lincoln and London

This volume in the Great Plains Photography Series is made possible by a grant from the University of Nebraska Foundation to extend the work of the University beyond its campuses.

A portion of "Driving on Gravel" first appeared in *Nebraska Humanities* 1, no. 3 (Summer 1991) as an expansion on the poem "Moving Day: Goodbye to the Big Elm," also appearing in that issue. "Above the Horizon: Cranes, Sunsets, Clouds" first appeared as "Cranes, Sunsets, Clouds: Just Looking in Nebraska's Sandhills" in *Sonora Review* 18 (Fall/Winter 1990)

The paper in this book meets the minimum requirements of American National Standard for Information Sciences – Permanence of Paper for Printed Library Materials, ANSI Z39.48–1984.

Library of Congress Cataloging-in-Publication Data
MacKichan, Margaret A., 1948–
In the kingdom of grass /
Margaret A. MacKichan,
Bob Ross.
p. cm. – (The Great Plains photography series)
ISBN 0-8032-3159-8 (cl)
1. Sandhills (Neb.) – Description and travel – Views.
I. Ross, Bob, 1944–. II. Title.
III. Series. F672.S17M33 1992
978.2–dc20 91-34853 CIP

Contents

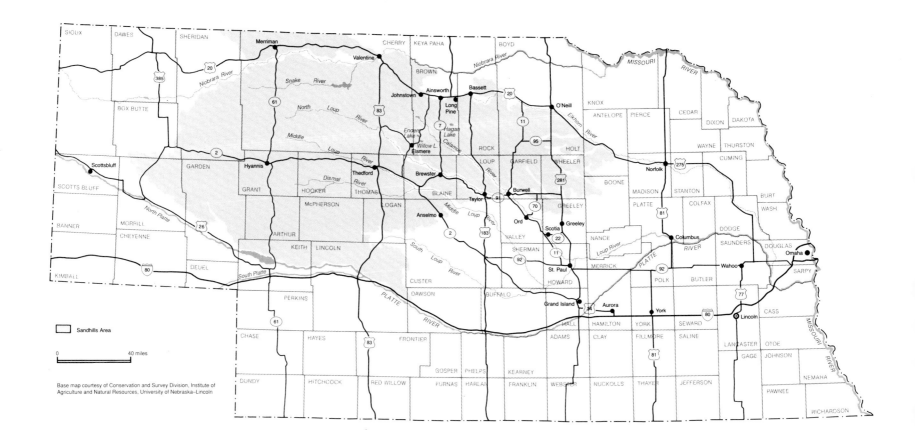

SIOUX | DAWES | SHERIDAN | CHERRY | KEYA PAHA | BOYD

Merriman

Valentine

Niobrara River

MISSOURI RIVER

BROWN

Ainsworth | Bassett | O'Neill

Johnstown | Long Pine | 20

KNOX | ANTELOPE | PIERCE | CEDAR | DIXON | DAKOTA

BOX BUTTE

Snake River

North Loup River

Enders Lake | Hagan Lake | Calamus

Elkhorn River

WAYNE | THURSTON

Middle Loup River

95

Willow L. | Elsmere

ROCK | HOLT

CUMING

GARDEN | Hyannis

LOUP | GARFIELD | WHEELER

Norfolk | 275

Scottsbluff

GRANT | Thedford | Brewster | BLAINE | Burwell | 281 | BOONE | MADISON | STANTON | BURT

SCOTTS BLUFF

Dismal River

HOOKER | THOMAS | Taylor | 70 | GREELEY | PLATTE | COLFAX | WASH

North Platte | McPHERSON | LOGAN | Anselmo | Ord | Scotia | Greeley | 81 | Columbus | DODGE | DOUGLAS

BANNER | MORRILL | CHEYENNE | 26 | 2 | 183 | 22 | NANCE | Loup River | Omaha

VALLEY | SAUNDERS | SARPY

ARTHUR | KEITH | LINCOLN | SHERMAN | 11 | Wahoo | 77

92 | St. Paul | MERRICK | PLATTE RIVER

KIMBALL | 80 | DEUEL | South Platte | South Loup River | HOWARD | POLK | BUTLER

Grand Island | Aurora | York | 80 | Lincoln | CASS

PERKINS | DAWSON | Platte River | BUFFALO | HALL | HAMILTON | YORK | SEWARD | LANCASTER | OTOE

61 | CHASE | HAYES | 83 | FRONTIER | ADAMS | CLAY | FILLMORE | SALINE | GAGE | JOHNSON

81 | MISSOURI RIVER

GOSPER | PHELPS | KEARNEY | NEMAHA

DUNDY | HITCHCOCK | RED WILLOW | FURNAS | HARLAN | FRANKLIN | WEBSTER | NUCKOLLS | THAYER | JEFFERSON | PAWNEE

RICHARDSON

☐ Sandhills Area

0   40 miles

Base map courtesy of Conservation and Survey Division, Institute of Agriculture and Natural Resources, University of Nebraska–Lincoln

About the Sandhills

The Nebraska sandhills are ancient sand dunes of mysterious origin that have been conquered and covered over by grass. They make an amoeba-shaped patch on the map of the state, extending northward to the state line north and west of Valentine and south to the Platte River and I-80. Their western edge crowds over into the Panhandle, the part of the state that lies above the northeast corner of Colorado, and an eastern lobe, topography which the geologists call "sand sheets," covers land south of the Elkhorn as far east as Boone County, straight south from where the Missouri River becomes part of the border. The sandhills make up about one-fifth of the state.

Because sand is porous, good at soaking up rain, several rivers rise in the sandhills: the North and Middle Loup, the Dismal, and the Calamus flow southward into the Platte, and the Elkhorn flows eastward, ending up in the Missouri. To the north, the Niobrara flows through the sandhills, picking up a major part of its volume there. The same sand that is good at accepting water is poor at holding onto it, so that for the most part—except for the river bottoms, and a few good scattered patches of sandy loam—it's a difficult soil to farm. The most consistently profitable use of the land has been the grazing of livestock.

Sandhills terrain differs from most other kinds in this respect: much of it is not dissected by a network of branching streams, streamlets, and gullies. Therefore, rainwater running down the side of a hill may eventually find itself in a lake, small pond, or "pothole," rather than in a creek. From there, it may evaporate directly; it may be transpired—sucked up by the lush water-loving vegetation of a sandhills meadow and used to turn sunlight into cellulose and sugar—or it may travel sideways and downward on a dark, slow, secret pathway through the porous earth. Over countless centuries, enough rainfall has taken this latter course to charge a reservoir of groundwater, the Ogallala Aquifer, that extends all the way to Texas.

Water that travels sideways through the earth may, if the slope of the land is steeper than the gradient of the groundwater, emerge into sunlight again at a lower elevation. This phenomenon accounts for the sandhills' character as a wetland. Exceptional rainfalls, rather than generating huge runoffs and downstream floods, simply fill every pothole and lake. If there is a dimple in the top of a hill, the water that fills it will soak in and may emerge at some distance, lower on the hillside, to help support a meadow. Even in dry years, the sandhills support some lakes; in wet years the number may increase tenfold as lands that were meadows become sloughs and—if seepage continues—open water.

Besides these "potholes"—ponds of an acre or less, which may last a month or a decade before vanishing without a trace, only to reappear the following spring or years later, after a torrential rainstorm—there is another feature characteristic of the sandhills and nowhere else. This is the "blowout," where the wind, with help from cattle or car tracks or gophers or rainwater, penetrates the thin sod and begins to move the sand grains. Somehow an edge is made, and a circulation is created, so that the wind swirls or rolls. The sand it carries begins to cut a wider and deeper trench, and the blowout is begun. Some of these get quite deep; what begins as a blowout during a dry cycle may turn into a pothole after a few wet years, and become a blowout again still later. Some blowouts are used as dumps, and this has spawned sandhills terminology: "Out to the blowout" signifies uselessness, as in "Someday I'm gonna hitch onto this damned ol' pickup and drag it out to the blowout."

Sandhill ranches vary in size from a minimum of around a thousand acres—a ragged living for a single person, hardly enough to keep a couple in decent clothes—on up to tens of square miles. The terrain varies, too, so that while in some parts a horse is unnecessary, in other places the land is rugged enough that cattle can outwit a four-wheel-drive. A third variable is distance from town. Near the larger towns, more and more ranch owners prefer city water and paved streets over country air and meadowlarks; if anyone lives out on the place, it will be a younger son or a hired man, someone not too particular about sweeping the floor or doing dishes. Farther from town, though, the driving back and forth becomes impractical, and the families who own and run the ranches still live on them.

A few years ago the average sandhills ranch contained four thousand acres. That's a lot of room to roam around on, but to put things in perspective, there are plenty of farms that size. (A farm, as distinguished from a ranch, is a piece of land where every clod of dirt, every year, gets picked up, turned over, and sprayed with something toxic. Ranchers only spray what's on top.) Ranching tends to be a business of high investment, where returns vary wildly according to market fluctuations; profits are unpredictable. Small ranches are always marginal, and the big ones are not exempt from bankruptcy. Some ranchers spend money when they have it, some spend money they don't have yet, and some never spend a nickel without protest; among the millionaires, it seems that the last type predominates.

Sandhills people regard themselves as stoic, independent, tough, and hospitable; by and large, they live up to these standards. It's a country where the old retain their authority, and where orneriness may be allowed considerable slack. Drinking is not unknown, and among those who indulge, "knowing when to say when" may amount to recognizing that the sun's coming up and it's Monday morning. It's a country of low wages, if you have to work for wages, and it's a long way to the hospital. The wind has access to everyone; egalitarian values apply, on the surface. The rich are there to show that anyone can get rich, and the poor believe it.

In the fall of 1975, a sandhills rancher and writer named Bob Ross struck up an acquaintance with a Lincoln photographer named Margaret MacKichan. He had visited the Sheldon Gallery and had very much admired a show of her work among the Appalachian people of Wolfe County, Kentucky; as they talked, he allowed that the people he'd grown up among were unusual, too, and might be worth an investment of her professional time.

Of her first visit to the sandhills, Margaret says, "I drove out with my camera to look around; stayed with a friend's mother in Anselmo, and visited her former schoolteacher, Niomia McGrew. Niomia was a widow, and still ran the 700 Ranch. Small by some standards, the 700 had eighty-four miles of fence to keep up. We bumped across the hills while she talked about blow-outs, windbreaks, bull wallows, and the winter of '49. She schooled me on ranch etiquette before turning me loose on branding day.

"On the basis of those photographs I was awarded small grants from the Nebraska Arts Council and Nebraska Committee on the Humanities to continue photographing. The Sandhills Cattle Association were my sponsors, and various members hosted me for weeks at a time. To be closer to my subject, I applied for a position as artist-in-the-community in Scottsbluff, through the West Nebraska Arts Center. The job was designed to let me spend two of every four weeks out on the ranches, an ideal situation.

"The ranch families good-naturedly allowed me to dog their tracks and photograph them until they became numb to the clicks. They fed my outdoors-whetted appetite, doctored my chilblained toes, pulled me out of snowbanks, and woke me at four to check the springer lots during calving. They allowed me to photograph their 'Okies' as well as their purebreds, and stopped the pickup on every hilltop knob between the Loup and the Niobrara to admire the view and the caked cattle below. They took me to dances and church, weddings and funerals. They shared the richness of the sandhills."

The result was a growing collection of photographs. Margaret began to think of a book, and decided that it might be well if some essays accompanied the photos. A poet she knew agreed to write the essays, but failed to come through, and the project threatened to collapse. In the meantime, Bob Ross left the country, first to study writing at the University of Montana and then to teach in Alaska. The summer of 1986, though, found him laid off and living on the ranch again; a talk with Margaret produced an offer. Would he write essays for her book? He would.

The two worked independently, agreeing that

neither would he caption her photographs nor would she illustrate his essays. Their views of the sandhills—even the subjects they covered—are different. We hope that the reader and viewer, combining these separate visions, may get a three-dimensional glimpse of this unique region. If the beauty and dignity of the land and its people come through, it is because beauty and dignity are there in abundance; if the combined portrait seems arid and uninteresting, the fault is with the authors. No matter how strong the light, it is always hard to see things clearly, and when we love a place it may be beyond our power.

About the photographs, Margaret MacKichan says, "Vast expanses of rolling hills rarely translate into two-dimensional images equally compelling. Everything has to be perfect for the landscape to be revealed; the contours and natural contrasts must be interesting and harmonious before the raking morning or evening sun can define them. The eye's bias is toward the land, but what is happening in the sky holds equal importance for the photographic image.

"While topography makes the sandhills unusual, it was the people who live and work those isolated holdings that drew me to photograph there. My interest lies in observing and interpreting the relationship between the land and the people whose lives are molded by it. Photographing expanses of land and sky requires light and timing, not to mention the 'eye' to give it order and meaning on the film plane. Portraiture is more complex: a cooperation, the spontaneous union of subject and photographer.

"The role of the portrait photographer is to bring out a person, to coax the subject to reveal him- or herself to the camera, then to be sensitive and recognize those inherent qualities. That alone, however, is not enough; the same considerations of light and dark, pattern and composition that apply to landscapes also apply to portraits. Photographing people in the midst of their lives requires a heightened awareness. All input is monitored, not simply the human content; these environmental elements further interpret who this person is and give a sense of 'rightness' to the image."

About the text, Bob Ross says, "These essays were supposed to be factual, but elements of fiction have crept in. In particular, two fictional characters have been introduced. 'Joe Carlsen' is a composite, sharing traits with several men I knew. The crotchety young writer in 'The Lost City' is a humorous portrait of myself of fifteen years ago, moved to a more recent time. I have taken other liberties with past and present tense. I have also, people tell me, simply gotten things wrong.

"I chose to write about a small part of the sandhills that I know through my own experience; not everything I describe is typical of the region. My writing is emotional, prejudiced, and flavored by ancient grudges and defeats. I've tried to be fair, and can only apologize where I've fallen short. A personal essay is personal. The reader must not look for science."

ACKNOWLEDGMENTS
The authors wish to thank the Nebraska Arts Council and the Nebraska Committee on the Humanities for their support in initially funding the photography, and the many banks and businesses which donated matching funds. Special thanks to the West Nebraska Arts Center and to Mike Shonsey, its director during 1978 and 1979, and to Bill Shopher for his help with the Scottsbluff businesses. Thanks also to the Sandhills Cattle Association, especially the Moreland families and Don McGuire, and to all the other families who shared their knowledge and their homes. This includes, of course, our own parents, Kenneth and Lois MacKichan of Lincoln, and Ed and Alice Ross of Ainsworth.

Thanks must also go to the National Endowment for the Arts, whose money helped support the essay part of the project, to Van Deren Coke, for his encouragement of the photographer over the years, and to the University of Nebraska Foundation for their grant in support of publication. Thanks to Lincoln photographers Roger Bruhn and Bill Ganzel for their assistance in sequencing the photographs. And, finally, our deepest gratitude goes to the people of the sandhills who have kindly permitted themselves to be written about and photographed. Without their patience and indulgence, there could be no book.

Driving on Gravel

My father has announced he would like to go to the ranch.

It's a clear day near the middle of July, a minute or two past ten o'clock. Earlier this month it was broiling hot, but now the weather has changed completely, behaving like a different summer. There's been rain. One night last week I had to turn the furnace on.

He picks me up (I have a house in Ainsworth, now) in his ten-year-old maroon Ford, sliding over so I can have the driver's seat. It's a nice car, sort of, an "executive car" that's been in a hailstorm. He got a deal on it, has had it six or seven years; the tappets sound pretty bad, but it runs. We drive to the Co-Op, fill it up with gas, and check the antifreeze. Last week, when I was in Lincoln, Dad drove to the ranch and back alone, but he knows I hate for him to do that. At eighty-four, he can slip off into napland any second. Boredom and a clean conscience, I guess.

We turn off the broad and quiet Main Street onto the highway, heading east past the Frontier and the Golden Steer, the S & S Store and the Hiway 20 Cafe. Dad rolls up his window, turns on the air conditioner (though to my mind it isn't warm), and lights a cigarette; I roll mine up too, so his smoke doesn't all drift past my nose. We ride quietly, each of us silent in his own preoccupations.

"Corn looks pretty good," I say. We're skirting the south edge of Buffalo Flats, some of Brown County's best farm ground. A center-pivot system makes a mist across the road.

"Some of it's tasseling already," he says. Like most older farmers, he says *toss*-el, not *tass*-el. "Should be taller. It got a slow start this year. If the weather doesn't straighten up, what was put in late's not going to make."

"Weather seems pretty nice to me," I say.

"Corn needs warm nights. This July it's either been too cool or it's been too hot." Dad never loses patience explaining things to me. If I'd been him I'd have given up years ago.

We pass the vet clinic and some newer homes, built out along the highway, away from town traffic and taxes. Enough "acreages" are scattered along here now that it almost resembles a country boulevard. Most are new and sprawly ranch-style homes, but on the left a tall peeling mansion among fallen outbuildings reminds the others that one generation's wealth can dwindle and disperse, leaving the next to its own partially apt devices.

East of the junction with Highway 183, we approach the Willow Creek and Pine Creek canyons. Before irrigation came to this country, Willow Creek was really only a draw, flowing during spring run-off and after heavy rains. Now it flows year round, almost as big as its neighbor. Pine Creek is more illustrious, boasting a couple of resorts, a state recreation area, and trout. When I was a teen-ager, the town of Long Pine piped its sewage into Pine Creek, the cascade known locally as "Piss Falls." Such things are no longer permitted. Pine Creek and its humble canyons are of interest to botanists and ornithologists; together with the Niobrara's canyons to the north, they are about as far east as the western conifer forest extends. Among bird species, eastern and western cousins sometimes mingle here, producing hybrids. Tourists headed up Highway 20 toward the Black Hills and Yellowstone get a teasing whiff here of the resinous air they're traveling to breathe.

Deer and wild turkeys live all along Pine Creek, but today I see nothing but a long-tailed black-and-white bird picking at a dead possum beside the road.

"Damn magpie," Dad says. I thought he was asleep.

When I was very small—we still lived in Johnstown, so I might've been as much as four—I remember hating the drive to the ranch. In my memory it was always hot; the prickly plush of the round-backed Chevy's seats was pungent with dust, and I was convinced I would be carsick. (My mother always brought along a coffee can, mostly for my morale since I don't remember ever having to use it.) I rode facing backwards, kneeling on the seat; being able to see outside seemed to ease my queasiness. The car was full of my father's cigarette smoke. Highway 20 was paved, so from Johnstown to Long Pine we were on asphalt. After the turn south it was gravel to the bullet-pocked "End of State Maintenance" sign, then clay, then sand. I remember there was one sandy hill on the last part of the trail that was always a struggle for the Chevy to get over. The trip, on a good day, must've taken an hour and a half.

Rolland, my cousin, lived at the ranch, along with his mother Grace, my Mom's younger sister, and Uncle Howard, who swung me high up and tickled until it hurt, and who sometimes gave me a teaspoon of minty schnapps. There was a baby sister, Jamie, whose diapers made the house pungent, and a pen of sheep in the ammonia-smelling barn. Rolly I liked pretty well as long as he did what I told him, but a mean dog lived there that I didn't care for, and why anyone would want a baby in the house was beyond me.

Later I collected sand turtles, demanding that Dad stop for every one we saw. We lived in Ainsworth by now, and my sandbox in the back yard stunk eloquently of turtle poop. I remember screaming with outrage as I spotted yet another black-and-yellow treasure and Mom, hoping against hope I'd believe I hadn't seen it, shoved my head below the level of the dash.

Rolly and Jamie and Grace and Howard moved to Long Pine and were succeeded on the ranch by the Masterses and the Severes, young couples looking for a fresh start, and by single men, Harry, Larry, Moe, Curly, and Joe. (I have changed these names.) Harry had an autogate (a row of pipes covering a trench; the government calls them "cattle guards") named after him because he always went to sleep on his way home Sunday night and missed it, plowing into the fence. Larry disappeared, leaving behind a graceful little Browning .22 rifle. Of course I hoped he was dead, but he was only up in South Dakota, so I didn't get to keep it. Moe likewise vanished but was discovered more quickly, shacked up a few miles from Johnstown, and I went with Dad to recover our pickup truck, which he had borrowed. On the porch of the house, two gunny sacks overflowed with empty beer cans. The truck's U-joints were out, so that it clanked and clattered all the way back to Ainsworth. Curly was a small, dark, active man who didn't drink or cause trouble, but he was useless with machinery, couldn't keep a clutch in the pickup when he was around, and Dad let him go.

Of the single men, Joe Carlsen was by far the most versatile. Dad hired him to run a hydraulic hay stacker after I tore up our old wooden one so badly it couldn't be repaired. (I was driving my uncle's John Deere tractor, backing up at the end of a heavy rope to slide the loose hay to the top of the stack. In a moment of fourteen-year-old inattention I simply pulled the middle pulley blocks sideways out of the stacker, along with every piece of lumber they were attached to, a feat that caused my father to stand in complete meditative silence for several day-long seconds.) Able to handle a horse, patient and savvy with cattle, and a wizard with

any kind of machinery, Joe took our remote and lowly ranch job only as a help in keeping sober. At different times and for different reasons he'd lost the fingers of his right hand, part of his stomach, and one of his testicles; besides these physical amputations, there were whole stretches of his life he couldn't remember, and he referred to his wife (though he lived a bachelor life on the ranch, he had a woman in Ainsworth) as "she" because he couldn't be sure he'd get her name right. He was full of smutty jokes and riddles and knew countless anecdotes of the misbehaviors of various upright citizens. He was the only bachelor for whom we felt respect bordering on friendship, and the only one Dad hired twice. Joe's personality curdled when he turned back to drink, though, and he in his turn was fired.

The road to the ranch underwent slow improvements. First the clay was extended, then covered with gravel, and the big sandy hill was circumvented. There were wet years when a causeway had to be built across a slough, then abandoned when the slough turned to a lake. Buildings along the road declined. In town life, my father sold real estate, so he knew the histories of all the "places" along the way; every time we drove the road he patiently repeated their names to me as we passed, and every time I gazed blankly in total disinterest, so that the only one I can name today is the "Duvall place," where a grove of box-elders and a corral remain.

I began driving on the meadow at the age of eight, and was sometimes allowed to drive the lower part of the road to Long Pine when I was ten. During the stormy winter I was sixteen, I had the job of hauling cottonseed-meal cake from Ainsworth to my Uncle Oz's place. I drove too fast and had poor luck navigating the constantly changing "snow road" across the hills, but with the help of generous neighbors, who winched me out of snowbanks week after week, I made my Saturday runs and the cows got fed.

For a couple of years after I got my license, I barreled over the gravel roads like a stock-car racer. Not like a real one, because I never rolled a vehicle, but I could make the run to Bassett for baler parts and be back in about an hour. There's a trick to driving on gravel, which is to push the car beyond a certain point of vibration, to where it floats smoothly over the washboard ridges and responds to the steering wheel more like a boat than an automobile. I only stopped doing this when I learned it was distance I wanted, not speed.

Recently Dad was grieving his brother Ozro, who died this spring at eighty-six, and he said, speaking of his younger brothers and sisters, "I was like a father to them—I did everything I could—and, one after another, I watched every single one of them leave." As my father passed through his teens, his own father was becoming mentally incompetent. Lyman, the oldest brother, left for college and a job in Chicago; the sec-

ond, Oz, quit school and went ranching on his own. While Dad stayed on and tried to keep the farm together, Oz married and moved to South Dakota, but he came back during the drouth-and-grasshopper years of the thirties. All the time I was growing up, Oz and Myra's place was just three miles across the hills from the ranch my parents owned. When I first returned to live on the ranch in 1972, they were still neighbors, but shortly afterward they sold out and moved here to Long Pine.

Missed by the highway and abandoned by the railroad, the town sits just out of sight, inviting travelers with a modest sign: "Welcome to Long Pine—Beauty Spot of the Sandhills." Main Street here is even broader and more deserted than in Ainsworth. I slow carefully to twenty-five—the Long Pine cop is death on speeders—and pass a couple of well-built older homes with beveled glass above their picture windows, three or four poorer houses in different stages of decay, and some nice split-levels; about a third have "For Sale" signs. Between Jeanie's Cafe and Shorty Mundorf's junk yard I turn left onto a gravel street. A block past the school, the street curves right and passes under a wooden railroad trestle; it emerges as a paved road again, albeit a narrow one, and we're out of town already. Just past the trestle, an enormous silver grain bin reflects the late-morning sun. Once Long Pine was a switching point on the railroad, and a roundhouse and switchyard and corrals for livestock filled the strip of land where the bin now sits. Black locomotives whuffed and hissed, chains of boxcars squealed and banged, and fat men in striped overalls waddled along the tracks. The roundhouse is the first of several landmarks that aren't here any more.

We're rolling quietly on asphalt, south past an alfalfa field on one side and cornfields on the other. The soil here is gravelly, not even good pasture until center-pivot irrigation came along. Someone with an eye for opportunity bought up a few sections, and now the corn reaches high as any.

My father is asleep now for sure. "This oil road sure is nice," I say, just to wake him up a bit.

"Sure is," he responds, as quickly as if I hadn't caught him napping. "I wish we'd had it twenty years sooner."

Past the alfalfa and cornfields, we round a slight bend and drop down into the Pine Creek canyon again, shallower here, the Jack Robertson place on the left. This used to be a zigzag sluice of deep and tricky gravel, with a narrow wooden bridge at the bottom, but the road has been straightened and the bridge replaced by a culvert. No more bridge planks clattering at midnight as some cowboy steers his way home from the Sunday night dance at Hidden Paradise. If we're going to see wild turkeys, we usually see them here, so I slow the car and look around. Nothing today but a hawk crossing the wind. We'll traverse this canyon one more time, in about a mile; it's hard to say exactly, but here's about where the sandhills proper begin. ∽

In the late spring of 1962, sometime around the middle of June, my Aunt Myra's nephew E. B. and I spent a few days camping at a place called "Phillips's Pond," a sandpit on the Calamus River south of Ainsworth. We would go there every year once school was out, to catch bluegills and bullfrogs, eat Campbell's cream-of-mushroom soup cold from the can, wade in the river, listen to the grass grow, and talk. At night we lay in the open, each of us under a tarp and blankets, swatting mosquitoes and gazing up at the stars. Already in 1962 there were stars that moved. Not the red-and-green airplane lights we were used to seeing, these were steady dots that crossed silently from one horizon to the other, along a line that was ever so slightly bent. Satellites. They had names like *Echo* and *Telstar*, and we watched their unearthly passages solemn with wonder.

I'd be a liar if I claimed to remember what we said. But watching those distant enchained lights surely made us ponder our own trajectories. I was going to be a scientist, I thought, maybe a physicist, though I did as well in chemistry. E. B. (he was called, like E. B. White, by his initials) was going to be a veterinarian. He could work with animals and at the same time make money, quite a departure from ranching as we knew it. He wanted cash for the things it could buy; he already owned a quartz watch, a bulging chrome thing that had cost him a hundred dollars and was advertised to be as accurate as the clocks used in launching satellites. A hundred dollars was big money to either of us, but his watch was the latest trick of pop tech and he was in love with it. Lights in the sky and a watch that kept time without ticking—from under dew-wet canvas, we looked up at a world glistening with marvels, starry with possibility.

That fall I left for the university at Lincoln. I found schoolwork difficult for the first time in my life; I found men who seemed utterly contemptible by my sun-baked standards to be professors whom I must find some way to respect. Instead of a stately rider in a dandelion meadow of stars, a satellite became an "x" whose velocity I must calculate given its distance from the Earth's center of mass. Swept in the hive of anxious energy and anonymous motion, striving for camouflage, I changed deeper than skin; I forgot my slow-wheeling sandhills summers, and became a stranger to the soft country of my youth.

Ten years later, in September of 1972, I was in Seattle, unemployed and living on my savings, when I got a call from Omaha. My father needed surgery and there was no one looking after the ranch. Could I help out for a couple of weeks? The request did not please me, but for a couple of weeks, I supposed I could. It took a day and a night to pack my books and clean my apartment; I weighed 155 pounds, less than I had in high school—I am six foot two—and such was the condition of my mind that when I saw northern lights above Couer D'Alene, I had to consider whether I

might be hallucinating. I crossed half the country in three days.

First my father was ill, then my mother. Then, at the end of September, the earliest snowfall in memory laid a thick white shawl across hills and meadows. Counting on the good weather usual at that time of year, Oz and Myra had made a quick trip to Colorado, so I had to travel by tractor to feed my uncle's stock. I got stuck when I left the ridge to cross a swale; I climbed down to shovel and found the snow dense with moisture, weighty as flesh. Underneath, where the bright sun shone through the drift, I sliced into pale turquoise, glacier color. I had never seen turquoise snow. Hot in my coveralls, soaked from the knees down and shaking with effort, I chopped at and cursed the beautiful stuff and learned how weak I'd become. When the turquoise snow melted away it was time to cable in the summer's haystacks. An axle snapped; I left the tractor in the field and made a trip to Lincoln for some used parts. Soft fingers bleeding, broomstick arms a-quake, I jacked and blocked it up, tilted the heavy wheel away, drained the grease, removed and replaced the bull gear, and when the old thing ran again I had a sense of accomplishment I hadn't felt in years.

When my parents returned from Omaha, they stayed in Ainsworth and left me to care for the ranch. That winter was not easy for me; I quit in February, forcing Dad to sell his cows, and went traveling for a month back to Seattle and then down to Tucson. My girl in Seattle had another man, my friends in Tucson had their usual interests and had not been troubled by my absence, and I found myself as much a stranger in those places as I was in my home town. I returned to Nebraska, settled into a deep loneliness, and began doing what I'd often said I meant to do, writing poetry. I wrote not about pain and politics and drugs and the trouble over Vietnam, but about wind and grass and calves and coyotes and tractors and turquoise snow, and the two weeks stretched into eight years.

"Pheasant."

Now it's Dad's turn to startle me. I slow down and study the ditch on his side of the car. A rooster snakes among the weeds, head and tail horizontal; he gives us the eye over his shoulder, as if he's of half a mind to kick our butts. A long time ago we had a bright red Rambler wagon with tailfins, and cock pheasants would ruffle their necks and crow, challenging us.

We've passed the Ed Stec place and the "school-house corner" (no schoolhouse; only an angle of cedars in the corner of the fence and the pipe that used to hold the teeter-totter remain) and are now winding gently through the hills on a good gravel road. This is grazing land, and my father perks up, taking an interest. He'll be watching as we pass to see how each pasture is holding up; his assessment takes into account not just the height and density of grass, but the proportion of good to poor grasses, their state of ma-

turity with respect to the season, and the particular rancher's grazing habits. He will notice how high up on the hills the cattle have grazed (like us, they won't climb if they don't have to) and whether they've worked the ends of pastures, away from the wells.

"Needle grass has dropped its needles," he says with satisfaction. "Looks like the grama's coming along." What's been a poor summer for corn has been fine for the pastures; there was plenty of rain in June, and the recent cool weather has helped the early-season grasses stay fresh. Past the Duvall place a chain of small ponds lines the west side of the grade; in dry times these disappear.

"Funny we haven't seen any ducks along here," I say. "These potholes were full of mallards two weeks ago."

"Mallard drakes molt around this time," Dad says. "They hide out in the grass because they can't fly. I'm not so damn sure they can swim. Can't float high in the water like a duck's supposed to, anyway."

Now the road branches into two narrow tributaries, southeast and west; we take the west. "The Y" is thirteen miles south of Long Pine, about seven from the ranch. A man who grew up on the place that later became Oz and Myra's told me there used to be a town here, but I think by "town" he meant a store and post office, probably in the same building. I can remember one narrow shed, long out of use, that slumped nearer to the grass each year. Farther along there's a little grove of shipmast locust, probably started from a single tree. It may have been planted for fence posts. All shipmast locust ever amounts to in the sandhills is a place for cattle to scratch and a home for ants.

We pass a windmill—a schoolhouse was here once, too, no traces at all of this one—and cross a sandy causeway at the edge of Macnamara Lake. The tires buzz over an autogate. "Looks like Mr. Forgey's getting some hay up," I say. This is a big ranch by our standards; the next four miles of road lie on one man's property.

"They're starting on the north end this year," Dad says. "Probably hoping the sloughs will dry up so they can cut them later on." He never responds to the mocking "Mistah" I customarily put in front of the man's name; it implies envy, and Pop has outlived envy for the most part. He considers the wealthy proprietor a better neighbor than some.

A white pickup is coming the other way. I pull over so my left wheels ride the right-hand track, and she does the same. It's Glenna, our neighbor on the north, a widow who runs a place similar in size to our own. She gives us a broad grin and a big wave, which I return. If two pickups pass each other in the ruts of a wet clay road, and one has a 1900-pound bull trying to climb out over the rack and the other driver has just dropped his cigarette lighter and set fire to his pants—they wave.

I once walked to the ranch from farther than this, back where the shipmast locusts were. There wasn't much

snow and the sky overhead was blue, but a forty-mile-an-hour wind had raised a ground blizzard and I'd come to a drift a hundred yards long. I backed up to a clear spot where the snowplow could pass, and shut off the engine. It wasn't particularly cold, I had warm clothes on, and I thought I ought to get home and feed my cows. The trouble was that the road was glazed with ice, and the wind kept knocking me down. Forgey's hired man had gotten a call from town and came out on the tractor looking for me; he took me to their headquarters where his wife made me hot chocolate, then drove me as near as he could get to our place, which left me with a mile to walk. When I finally got home I was too tired to feed; I called my folks to let them know I was OK, ate a hot dog and went to bed. The next morning I was awakened by the snowplow man, knocking on my door to ask if I wanted a ride to my truck.

The longest I was ever snowed in was five days. The road gets muddy, too; three years ago I was living down here in the spring, and the water started coming up. My options got closed down to where there was only one way out, a long and winding detour to the south and west, ending up on Highway 7 south of Ainsworth. Back when this road was mostly clay, it was even worse. My mother hated riding over it when it was wet; she would clench her teeth and assist my father at every swerve by will power and a constrained body English. Getting anywhere was slow business then, and for every mile forward the car seemed to go two miles back and forth across the road.

Oz and Myra used to have a huge stockpile of books and jigsaw puzzles. Aunt Myra was a vicious card player—still is—and she and E. B. shared a family pastime of recreational arguing, preferably over some trivial fact like the origin of Jell-O. People expected to be isolated at times; they had ways to keep from going crazy. Radio must've been a great help when it came, and television is considered essential now. Satellite dishes bring in shows and commercials filmed in New York and Los Angeles; faces more familiar than those of relatives are as close as the remote control, and no one thinks of digging out a fifteen-year-old jigsaw puzzle. Arguing doesn't seem like fun any more. Once in a while, though, the TV gets switched off. Someone looks out the window and sees a deer.

We're passing Forgey's buildings now, the first house visible since the Stec place, about ten miles. We've gone by the slough with the Canada geese—didn't see them this time—and have been passed by an unfamiliar pickup truck loaded with furniture. It's only three miles to where we're going, though the road loops on. There's always a little rise of the heart when we cross over the last autogate and onto our own property. We'll look around a little, do a little snooping, then go back to town. The pastures are leased; they should be haying the meadow. It's curious how little we have to do with it all. I always like coming here, and I'm never sorry to leave. The sky's bright blue, the air is cool. It's a pleasure driving on gravel now; most of my roads these days are paved to the horizon.

Right through here, on the Forgey place east of the buildings, one time there were about a million small yellow butterflies, doing something on the road: butterfly road work. I was going to Ainsworth that day, I forget just why, in my old green truck so comically full of dents. I slowed to a crawl, barely idling along, and the butterflies flew up ahead of me and settled back down behind, a butterfly blizzard. It was warm and muggy and the tires splashed water in the road, and the sawgrass and sweet clover that lines the ditches hadn't yet been cut. As I crept along like a float in a parade, I put my hand out the window and grinned and waved as though I'd become a celebrity.

By then I knew I had to leave; something I had to try required me to be elsewhere. Before I went, my father blessed me thus: "Son, when you first came home that time, we were concerned about you. But now I think you'll live to be an old man with a lot of regrets."

Poppa, here's my blessing for you. May the road you dream be sweet with clover. May the sky be blue, may sunshine gently warm your bones, and may you lift your hand to the applause of butterflies.

Above the Horizon: Cranes, Sunsets, Clouds

                When
                    cranes
                        honor
                            you,
                                flying
                                    near
                                        our
                                            home,
                                        look
                                    up.

                        Love,
                    do
                you
            miss
        me.

—To Fu (1292–1536)

I have friends farther west who, when reminded where I'm from, smile and glance at me in a puzzled way. I heard it spoken kindly by a very wide-eyed, pretty young woman at a New Year's Eve party in Santa Barbara. The conversation had turned to the plains states, and the inevitable lull followed. "I was in Kansas once," she put in. "Funny place. Kind of flat."

Kind of a devastating summation. Yet, when I'm driving in Nebraska's sandhills, I never consider scenery, or the lack of it, a problem. For one thing, my eye roves the grass, the haystacks and road ditches, cruising for birds. Grouse and prairie chickens live in the hills year-round, as do a few pheasants, meadowlarks, English sparrows, and owls. Most other birds come and go, but they do so in numbers and variety rarely to be found except along the ocean. In winter, when pickings are slim, chickadees from farther north prod the bark of the cottonwoods; a surly remnant of crows carry on crow business, lawyering the knife-edged air. By late spring, the skies are swarming.

Most people associate regions of sand dunes with deserts. It is certainly true that in parts of the sandhills, in a dry cycle, it can be miles to the nearest surface water. Further, the only force available that can scoop out a basin for a lake to fill is the wind, and wind can carry only dry soil, so it follows that the deepest sandhill lake must have been a gigantic blowout once. In fact, the sandhills provides, in aggregate, one of the largest wetland habitats in the inland U.S.

On the smaller lakes and marshes, mallards, pintails, and blue-winged teal thrive, along with a few "spoonbills" and a dowdy abundance of mudhens. Redwinged blackbirds screech in the reeds, killdeer and plovers busy themselves along the shore. A blue heron may stalk the shallows. Once, mowing along a lake, I uncovered a nest of "shitepokes," a tan wading bird, shorter than a heron, with stripes down its neck. I tried to herd the two nestlings toward standing rushes, and can tell you that nothing in the world could be uglier, dumber, clumsier-footed or more belligerent than a baby shitepoke. Some sandhill lakes are very nearly permanent. These deeper waters support fish and the birds that feed on them: pelicans, cormorants, gulls. Yellow-headed blackbirds prefer these lakes, and there is now a resurgent population of Canada geese. It is mostly to these lakes that the autumn migrants come, where they can raft up in open water more than a shotgun's range from shore.

The birds I love best are famous travelers, the sandhill cranes. (Sadly, they seem to be misnamed, for they nest in Canada and spend their winters in Texas.) They pass through twice a year; like tourists who always use the same route and stop at favorite cafés, they visit our ponds and meadows, liking places where there is water nearby but where the grass has been grazed or mowed. They prefer the finest weather or the worst, their squeaky-saxophone honks either drifting sweet and faint from great height on crisp cloudless days, or coming loud and mysterious from low clouds when a hundred-foot slant of drizzle is all that separates sky from ground. In late evening, grown weary with altitude, they spiral slowly down, very particular as to their landing field, and then you never heard such democracy at work. Music to both eye and ear, they glide in circles, debating, changing their collective mind again and again, to light finally at some insignificant

marsh just over the hill from the hopeful observer, who stands, mouth open, useless binoculars in hand, and watches the remainder of the sunset, vowing to rise in time to see them in the morning. But the birds always wake up earlier.

Once, only once, I was even further honored, on an early morning in spring, a socked-in day when no planes were flying. Our meadow lies in a sort of valley that runs north and south, and the clouds were down to the neighbor's fence on the high hill to the east. Up the valley, south to north, just under the dirty-cotton clouds, flew nine gangly, enormous, gleaming white birds. I swear they had the black tips on their wings: whooping cranes. I happened to be outdoors, and I saw them. I felt singled out, chosen, one in a million.

I've tried to put my feeling for the cranes into poems. My best attempt so far comes to just seventeen syllables; I type the words out one to a line down the middle of the page, to form sort of a straggled *V*. In America, sad to say, haiku is a form best left to grade-school children and to those who have retired from teaching them. Fortunately the cranes make their own poetry.

I confess I know a great deal more about sunsets than I do about sunrises. From the few I've witnessed, I'd say that sunrises tend to be less dramatically orchestrated and shorter, more like chamber music than a full-scale symphony. A good midsummer sunset starts half an hour before the fireball touches the horizon and blazes spectacularly through cloud-shifts and color changes, purpling and then fading until, impossibly far north, the last blue-green glow is quenched in moonlight. Evening thunderheads are lit up pink as roses, while the dusk deepens and palomino lightning gallops among the cloud-tops.

The clouds of sunrise are clouds that have passed; they kneel to the sun, their backs to the lingering darkness. It is sunrise that has been given Easter symbolism, eternal life said to follow death as day follows night. Sunsets remain unchristianized, Aztec, wilder than Wagner. "Wester" would be a rage of departure, like Mardi Gras combined with Halloween.

In winter, when there are no dramatic clouds, sunset may still be spectacular. When it is very cold and the weather clear, there are apt to be high cirrus clouds or ice crystals that carry a red-gold haze completely around the horizon, while the sky may blend from deep blue overhead toward a west of pale metallic green. The haloing effect is greatest when wind-packed snow armors the earth in glittering white all the way to where the sun goes down, somewhere in Wyoming.

In country life, watching the sunrise is seldom much of an option. Sunset, coming at the end of the day, is more accessible. There is something about the stubborn, darkening color that corresponds deeply to weariness in the bones and a sense that tasks are endless and life is short.

On my uncle's place we knocked off work at six o'clock, no matter what, and started chores. There were about twenty cows to milk, bucket calves to feed, and a quarter-mile of sprinkler pipe to be moved. Work was usually divided, with teen-age nephews consigned to the milk barn and younger and shriller nieces carrying pipe. Once the main milking had been done and calves and cats and pigs were being fed, there were intervals when a boy could stand idle, looking west to the glory beyond the trees. This was the only quiet time and the finest hour of the day. Supper eaten, we sometimes returned outside to bat June bugs or play Annie-eye-over in the dusk, but we were reticent and listless by then and the best of the light had gone. Instead of playing outdoors, I often read late into the evening, exploring a crumbling mountain of paperbacks in the attic, where you could find anything from *Comanche John* to *A Summer Place*, from Ray Bradbury to Somerset Maugham. When I turned out the yellow light and stumbled to the bunkhouse under a net of stars, I imagined I could float with the owls across the fields, or walk up the side of the bunkhouse and into the sky.

It's not easy to find something to say about sandhills cloud scenery that is neither obvious nor grandiose.

Obvious: clouds hold terrors and promises. Most of Nebraska's summer rains come from *cumulonimbus*, giant flatiron grumblers that glide ominously eastward on hot afternoons and evenings. Usually beneficial, often capricious, these thunderheads can pour out hailstones, blast the earth with lightning bolts, flatten crops with horizontal downpours and uproot trees and buildings with tornadic winds. Or, time after time, they can pass maddeningly overhead, leaving nothing behind but random sprinkles and the smoke of prairie fires.

While a boy, my grandfather was riding in the box of a wagon when lightning struck, killing the driver and a mule; my mother inherited lightning-fear from him. Mom herself had seen a brother, leaning against a brick chimney in a storm, knocked down by lightning. She had lived in Johnstown when a tornado went through (I think I remember this, a lot of whistling and cold drafts in the house) and in any case was an anxious person whom anxiety hurt physically, so that she would draw in air between her teeth: "Ssssp!" Our house was stocked with candles, a kerosene lamp or two, and battery radios, and when thunder came to call it was a wakeful place. My parents and I would meet in the kitchen, two steps from the basement stairway, drink coffee and listen to the rain.

As a teen-ager I loved thunderstorms, but when I returned a decade later to live alone on the ranch I developed something of my mother's terror of them. Partly it had to do with differences between town and country. In a city or town, the community's electrical system is grounded in lots of places, so that lightning usually can strike without causing much damage. In the country, where grounds are comparatively sparse, strange things happen. A ten-foot arc can snap between an electrical outlet and the nearest faucet; this is unnerving, even when you're in another room. The first telephone line to the ranch was a makeshift, and lightning had a habit of blowing the receiver off the wall. During one of my summers out at Uncle Oz's, I hung a radio above my bunk in the old schoolhouse, plugged into 200 feet of buried extension cord. On a weekend when I was in town a storm hit; E. B., my bunkhouse-mate, who happened to be reading in the iron bed next to mine, reported that a little ball of fire came out of the radio and floated to the foot of my bed. When I opened the radio, there were some burned-out components and the smell of plastic, but it continued to work fine. Only the tone had changed; it seemed scratchier, or maybe just a little tense.

Grandiose: clouds outtop the proudest mountains, the tallest thunderheads towering fifty or sometimes sixty thousand feet; nine or ten miles, high as jets. No mountain stands so lofty as to be barren of snow, which must fall from clouds. Storm clouds appear solid as granite and in fact weigh thousands of tons more than empty sky, that weight of water and ice held aloft by rising air currents. Rains of an inch an hour are infrequent but hardly rare; an inch of rain over an acre—less than a city block—is something like 36,000 gallons or 144 tons. An 80-by-120-foot suburban lot would catch 800 cubic feet of water, over 48,000 pounds, just about a semitrailer load. Imagine an eighteen-wheeler floating above your roof. Now, imagine one over every house in your neighborhood. In your town.

A lazy man's way to watch clouds is to look at the satellite scan on your nightly weather report. If they "put the weather into motion," you'll see continent-wide movements, swirls and waves, battenings and vanishings. Occasionally you may see the tips of the Rockies outlined, or a hurricane with its blind eye sweeping toward the coast. A better way to look at clouds is to be eight years old; lie flat on the ground next to your school or any tall building, with the top of your head right against the bricks, and gaze upward. As clouds pass the building's edge you'll feel the earth turn, and be as smart as Columbus. A farmer's way to see clouds is to stand on your back porch after supper and watch helplessly as a black-green bruise covers the sunset, while your wife's good boysenberry pie turns to splinters in your stomach.

Clouds are both commonplace and other-worldly; they drift and accumulate like a debt almost forgotten, some stern consequence gathering in the corner of the eye. They move in a sphere beyond our influence, lanterned by the inward balancing of immeasurable powers. They are weightless and freighted, tenuous but rending, harmless to nighthawks, deadly to planes. Their verticals, puffs, bulges, cornices, shades, glows, colors and blacknesses stun the eye, finally, to boredom. Though they dwarf our labors, they can merely veil the stars.

In April, in calving time, I used to walk the springer pens without a flashlight. (I carried one, but wouldn't flick it on unless I had to.) Because I would rise from sleep to do this, my eyes were attuned to darkness. On clear moonless nights, the sky seemed to be not a black lid but an ocean of faint blue-white, like skim milk diluted with ink, lighter far than the flat black earth. It was on one of these nights that I first saw rips in the firmament, slashes of emptiness that raked across the sky. Nothing in mind, sleepy head swimming, I watched until I saw the patches move. Dark seaweed floated on an ocean of light, slow as time itself; waves of cirrus were traversing the sky. It was a sight as profound as any cloud-vision of the daytime, disturbing and thoroughly beautiful. Five miles away, on Highway 7, a trucker changed gears to pull a hill; a few feet in front of me, a pregnant cow shifted, belched, and began to chew her cud. All of us living were sparks on a field of blackness. I looked up in innocence until my own thoughts gathered, condensed, and drifted to obscure my face.

Fence

Fencing is agreeable enough, as are most ranch chores, but the obligation of it weighs like leaden shoes. Pasture contracts start the first of May, and most ranchers "turn out" between May 15th and June 1st; fences should be up and tight so that the cattle, who make it their first duty to investigate the fence, stay where they belong. I don't start fixing fence until April (after all, we *could* have a late storm, and nothing takes down wire worse than the heavy snow of spring), and I don't go early in the day; I don't fence at all if it isn't pretty weather. I throw a dozen posts and the post-hole diggers in the back of a pickup truck, get the bucket of staples and a hammer and fence pliers, reach the Goldenrod wire stretchers down from their nail. I find a pair of gloves that are already ripped and drive out to one of the pastures. If I work it right, I'll run out of posts and quit around four o'clock.

In principle, one fences to keep one's own cattle "in"; that is the law in the state of Nebraska. In practice—provided the neighbors aren't thieves—keeping others' livestock "out" is as often the problem. Two brothers to the south of me used to have a fine old Angus bull who dropped in for a visit every spring; they always came and got him when I called, fixing the wire he had disregarded, and it was comical to see them leading him home, one of them sitting on the tailgate of the pickup rattling a Folger's can of cattle-cake. All the same, I wished he'd kept his nose out of my heifer pasture, because his timing was wrong.

Anyway, here we are. I've come through a couple of gates (no need to get out of the truck, the pasture gates lie open this time of year) and am driving at walking speed alongside the fence. For ranch work it's helpful to have a pickup with an extra gear on the low end; I drive along with the engine idling, reach out with the hammer handle, and give each post a good poke as I go by. It sounds lazy not to walk, but if I have to replace a post I've got them with me.

Our fences contain several kinds of posts; the oldest, and the most likely to need replacing, are white cedar, probably from Minnesota or Canada, and eastern redcedar, one of the tree species native to Brown County. (Redcedar heartwood is commonly used to make bridal chests and "moth-proof" closets. White cedar is familiar as decorative rail fencing; the wood is soft, coarse-fibered, and when sawed through it has a balsamy aroma.) The farm that Dad grew up on was finally lost to debt in 1942; before leaving, my father took off every cedar tree big enough to make a post, and when he and my mother moved to the ranch in March of 1943, his first job, once the ground thawed, was to begin building fence. That makes some of these little redcedar posts, often not two inches across, near fifty years old. Truth be told, there aren't many left, but they've done good service. White cedar rots away to a dull point; the only ones left now have broken off once and been reset, top end in the ground. With redcedar, the sapwood disintegrates, leaving the heartwood core to hold the post upright—if nothing leans on it—for an extra twenty years.

Two more old kinds of posts, cussed when encountered, are oak and osage orange. Scrub oak grows along the Niobrara and its tributaries, and makes fairly long-lived posts; sometimes the big ends are charred to help keep them from rotting. Oak posts are distinguished by their dark-gray, crumbly, wormshot appearance. Osage orange or "sage" posts are trucked from Oklahoma and Texas, where the tree is known as "bowdark," or *bois d'arc.* The big straight ones are virtually eternal and correspondingly expensive. Dad once bought a load of the smallest, two to four inches across and "so crooked you had to screw 'em into the ground." Most of them are still screwed in, but they're no one's favorite. Osage orange turns out to be nearly impossible to drive a staple into, and the tiny posts must be steadied against the palm of your hand, so your left hand stings as if you'd hit a baseball with the shank of the bat.

The next oak post I poke with the hammer handle swings back and forth like a "howdy hand" in the rear window of a psychedelic VW bus. Here's a case of the wire holding the post up, rather than vice versa. I turn off the pickup motor and listen for a moment to the jabbering of a Western kingbird—Dad calls them "bee martins"—a rod or two down the fenceline.

First I pull the staples and put them in the bucket. (I make it a rule never to spend more than fifteen minutes hunting for a dropped staple.) Fifty-year-old oak posts make wonderful firewood, so I toss this one into the pickup box. Next I get out the post-hole diggers. The kind we use has two handles (in Montana, where the soil is 85 percent rocks, a one-handled type with a sort of boulder-scooping lever is preferred). I begin digging by holding the handles as wide apart as they'll go (the blades therefore together) and stabbing the sod, taking out little wedge-shaped chips. Looks silly, but it's the correct technique for getting through the first inch or so. After that, I hold the handles together, stab, pull them apart, and raise the blades, lifting the soil out of the hole.

Once the sod is pierced, the digging takes two or three minutes. At first, it's pleasant exercise; the sand has a fine cool texture and a clean-earth smell, and I get a hint of the blue world's suburbs: root life, grub life. I go down two and a half feet, piling the sand near the hole—some of it always falls back in and has to be dug out twice—and get a new creosote post and the tamper, a slender axle from some ancient spidery automobile. I hold the post so it just touches each of the wires, and begin kicking and tamping the sand back in. (Here's an oddity: if there were loose, absolutely dry sand nearby—no cohesion, the Lawrence of Arabia stuff—I could put that down the hole instead of the moist sand I've just dug up. I'd simply wiggle the post and pour the dry sand in, and it would set up tighter than I could tamp it.)

A fellow who used to ranch along Plum Creek would cut a pickup-load of cedar posts, haul them to town, and sell them. Then he'd use the money to buy just half as many creosote posts, which he'd take back home to set in his fence. Creosote posts are pine poles that have been peeled, cut into lengths, and pressure-treated in a vat of licorice-colored carcinogenic goo. Their durability depends on whether the poles are dried after they're cut, how well the creosote penetrates the wood, and the concentration of the mix. Similar to creosote posts are tan or yellowish "penta" treated posts. They were a lot nicer to handle than creosote, cost and lasted about the same, but the stuff they were dipped in was so deadly that the EPA won't let them be manufactured any more. A new greenish copper-treated post is being sold to those who don't like the way creosote ruins their clothes, gloves, and skin, but there is some skepticism as to whether they'll last. Untreated pine lasts maybe five years; a green hackberry limb I once set rotted off in a year.

I've set the post so it barely touches each strand; this is curiously important and worth some trouble, because the straighter the fence the easier it is to stretch wire. Next, I staple the wire to the post; nothing very technical here. There's a place below my knee that feels right for the bottom wire, a place on my hip that's about right for the top, and the middle wire goes be-

tween. (Four-wire fence—most of our perimeter fence now has four wires—requires different spacing, which I have to measure with the hammer handle.) The fence my father bought with the land mostly had just two wires; it takes a despondent and unimaginative cow to be kept in by a two-wire fence. In the first year and a half, Dad built most of the corrals and nearly all of the cross fences, setting every post he'd brought with him and buying more. He, my mother, and my mother's father also built a pole barn and a five-room house, all this with a war on, materials hard to come by, and hardly any money. There was also the usual business of running livestock, trying to get the ranch going. Conceived near the middle of this wad of work, it's a wonder I wasn't born with a backache.

I throw the diggers and the tamper in the pickup, dust my hands, start the motor, and proceed along the fence, poking posts with the hammer as I go. It doesn't pay to be too particular; if there's a bit of sound wood left, that's good enough. Once when I was little I went out with a cousin to "help" my Uncle Oz fix fence. He sent us ahead of him to find the broken posts, unstaple the wire from them, and lay them down; he would come along and set new ones. He wondered why he was having to put in so many new posts, until he caught sight of the two of us, far ahead of him, one on each side of the fence, rocking back and forth. We were breaking off every post that seemed to make a cracking sound when we tested it. He ramped and roared, but we were too far away to hear. One thing about it, that section of fence didn't need much attention for years.

As I approach the crest of a knoll I notice slack in the wires, and when I get to the top I see that in the swale below me two of them are broken. I coast down the hill, looking around first to be sure I can drive out again; my pickup doesn't have four-wheel drive. This time when I shut it off a meadowlark salutes me: *per-twee-oop-whee-wheedlydeediddle.* Something like that. A cloud the shape of Paul Harvey's head is traversing the sky from the northwest.

Little flakes of snow have broken this fence. What happens is that wind blows snow off the ridges and into the low places, where it drifts. Snow is denser in a drift than when it first falls, because as the flakes rub and rattle along, their corners get knocked off. If it stays cold and the wind changes, blowing this way and that, the fluffiest white stuff will pack down into drifts a cow can walk across. When the weather warms up, this hard-drifted snow settles and sags, taking the wire downward as it goes. The wire stretches until it breaks, nearly always at the foot of a hill, where the drift is deepest.

All three wires have broken here before. The top wire, which is very old, has given way at the end of a previous splice; the splice on the second wire has held, but the wire itself has broken at the nearest staple. The bottom wire's not broken, but it needs stretching. I get the stretchers and fence pliers and a piece of loose wire from the pickup box and go to work. First thing is to loosen staples on the nearby posts; where the wire broke at a staple, I pull the staple and put it in my pocket.

Next thing is to stretch the fence. I start with the bottom wire and attach the stretchers across the old splice. The wire stretchers have a toothed jaw at each end that's supposed to catch the wire, and these get pounded tight with the fence pliers. Now I work the lever to tighten the wire. This is a delicate matter; you don't want the fence to break in another spot, and you don't want the ratchet mechanism to slip back and pinch you. Banjo-tight barbed wire is said to sometimes curl back on breaking and whip itself around you. Though I've never had this happen, I'm always a little nervous when I put tension on the stuff.

Once the fence is snug and I'm sure the jaws are holding, I undo the splice. To an electrician or a trout fisherman, this "splice" would be a crude joke; it's nothing but a foot-long piece of wire with loops at each end attaching it to equally unesthetic loops at the ends of the broken wires. I stretch the wire tight, stopping to wiggle the barbs through the old loop, and then re-bungle the splice. Some men pride themselves on making small, tidy loops; I make big ones, the size of a tablespoon. That way I won't have to untwist both loops next time. This bottom wire is still pretty flexible, so there's no trick to splicing it.

The middle strand is inferior, lightweight wire, maybe bought during the depression or World War Two; it's hard to tell just how old it is. Instead of splicing right at the post, I snip off a foot or two with the fence pliers and put in a length of new and heavier wire where the staple will go. That way, next time it'll break somewhere else.

The top strand is . . . well, people collect this stuff. Once, a white-haired man in an old green Chevy stopped and asked me for a piece of my fence. I said sure, hoping he'd roll up half a mile of rusty old wire and replace it with new, but he only wanted a couple of feet. Modern barbed wire has two-pronged barbs, but these barbs have four points each, and the wire itself is of a heavier gage; now a rind of rust surrounds what's left of the steel, making it even fatter. This ancient, brittle wire is the reason for my habit of making splices with big loops. Sometimes it helps to bend it around a hammer handle; sometimes you have to try three or four loops, progressively farther back, before you get one that won't break on you. Today, though, I'm in luck. This particular wire feels "soft"—bends easily—and old wire that has a soft feel usually splices well. This is no exception, and soon I'm stapling the wires back to the post.

When the land was first fenced, a hundred years ago, it must have been fine business for the steel companies. The earliest barbed wire came in a lot of styles and was mostly vicious-looking stuff, made for fencing "out" at a time when Texas steers could live four or five years and grow to weigh a thousand pounds without ever seeing a fence. They tried razor-ribbon wire and single-strand wire with sharpened spurs welded to it; nearly all of it was of a heavier gage than what's used now. Early cowboys hated the wire passionately and with reason. Horses, unlike cattle, will panic and fight the wire if they become entangled, and a wire-cut colt is a sickening sight. Imagine the harm that old razor wire might have done.

One more thing needs mending here, I see. At the bottom of a valley you need something to tie the fence down, because as the wire is tightened it tends to pull the posts up out of the ground. To hold it at the bottom, something called a "dead man" is used. A tire or any handy piece of junk is buried a couple of feet in the ground, and a vertical wire fastens the fence to it. Here the tie-down wire has broken; I make a loop, attach a new piece, start the pickup, and drive off, poking posts.

I've mentioned bee martins' gabbiness, and a barn swallow on a wire in the evening can be quite loquacious, but my candidate for champion chatterbox is the cowbird. That's what I hear when I stop the engine next. A bit smaller than a robin, this character is the color of scuffed black leather, or, not so fashionably, week-old cow manure. He compensates for his south-of-the-tracks accoutrements by charming his lady love with talk; this one does go on, hovering in the air, clicking and whirring and twittering like a small-town telephone exchange. Though we deem her drab, the female cowbird expects a glib approach. The reason I sit and stare so gloomily on such a warm blue breezy cowbird-chattered day is that I've come to the section line, and find that the cross-fence's corner has pulled out.

Like the cornerstone of a building, the corner of a fence is that on which all else depends. Cantilevered in the ground, it resists the pull of three or four (or six or eight) taut wires. This force is sustained year after year, and over that long a period soil behaves more like silly putty than like bricks. Therefore, in order to hold, a corner post must be big; it must also be set deep, it should have an anchor (a board or two nailed cross-ways near the bottom), and it must be braced. What's happened here is that the big old cedar post has come vertically part-way out of the ground. It's huge, full of knots and bumps so that you'd think nothing could uproot it, but there it is, the fat gray top looking embarrassed with its knobby pink underparts exposed. Though it seems heavy and strong, it's been in the ground longer than I've been on top of it, so here's one for the firewood pile once I get the wire unwrapped.

First I pull all the staples I can dig out, including the ones on the brace post. Once that's done, it's a matter of mind over barbed wire. The fence has been restretched to this corner countless times, and wire that was already old when this post was set has been untwisted and rewrapped each time, with the result that it has broken and been spliced, and now the splices are part of the wrap, loops and all. Prickly stuff. It springs loose suddenly, snatching at my shirt and gloves (piece of advice: wear a long-sleeved shirt to fix fence). As I get each wire loose, I walk it aside, several steps from where I'll be working.

Next step is to remove the brace wire. This is "number-nine" wire, hard, obstreperous steel, part of a sort of box truss arrangement that ties the brace post to the corner. You have the corner post, the brace post about six feet away, and an "x" between them with a crossbar at the top. The crossbar and one of the "x" pieces are wood, either posts or two-by-fours; the number-nine wire forms the other leg of the "x." It is looped around the outsides of the two posts, then twisted tight at the two open places by inserting a stick across the loop and winding the wire against itself, tensioning it to the breaking point. From an engineer's point of view, the idea is to make the corner and brace into a solid unit, so that the corner responds to the force of the fence by wanting to rise vertically rather than lean. This idea gets translated into actual fence corners with varying degrees of accomplishment, and not all corners look like the one I've described.

(After the telephone company switched from high lines to buried cable, there was a bonanza of corner posts and corral poles around here; they pulled up all the phone poles and left them lying in the hills, some only two or three years old and a foot thick at the butt, ready to be dragged in behind a tractor and chain-sawed. The one I'm about to set is the last of those, so I suppose I'll have to start buying corner posts again. They're expensive suckers, too.)

Next I dig out the old corner. I do more digging than you'd think necessary. This post weighs maybe forty pounds, not all that much, but if two knobs of cedar rub against opposite sides of the hole, I'll be trying to lift the ground under my feet as well. There's no elegant way to lift it; squat, wrap both arms around it, grunt. A chiropractor can do pretty well in ranch country. Folks who are serious about fencing usually own a tractor with a loader on the front and a power-takeoff-driven auger mounted in back. A swag of chain hangs from the loader bucket; a wrap around the post, a hiss of hydraulic fluid, and the post is out. Sensible. A few years back, my father and I pulled up a mile of posts in a couple of hours; Dad drove the tractor, ran the Farmhand loader, and smoked cigarettes, and I walked ahead and whipped the log chain over each post as we came to it. It was easy walking, and it made us a good day because it seemed like we were getting a lot done. That was about the last time we did an afternoon's ranch work together.

I take another bird break, but all I hear this time is the distant rumble of an airliner, five or six miles overhead. Sometimes National Guard fighters play tag fast and low over these hills; usually you won't see them coming or hear them until the jet noise hits you as they blast overhead. Here's another scary flying critter, a bumblebee. Western kingbirds are called "bee martins" because they catch bumblebees and eat them, holding them down on a fence post and thoroughly hammering the life out of them. Once while mending fence I found a mallard hen's nest, high on a hill and a long way from water, in the tall grass of the fencerow. I guess if you're born a mallard duckling, you have to walk before you can swim. Won't need to walk far if a hawk sees you.

All I have to do now is reconstruct the corner. I've got a corner post in the truck; I'll need to find something to nail crossways at the butt for an anchor (the old knobby cedar post didn't have one). I dig the hole a little larger, set the post, tamp it, saw a brand-new fence post to replace the gray two-by-four across the top, and notch the corner a bit to hold the down brace. Now I loop some number-nine wire and twist it, and I'm almost done. I've got the fence wires to re-stretch, and then I can take the rest of the day off.

Funny, it's almost supper time. The sun's butter-yellow and the warm spring day is cooling a little. On my way across the pasture I chase up a flock of prairie chickens, and they wing and glide, wing and glide toward the hay meadow, leading me home. My old green truck purrs softly, until I slam across a cowpath and it rattles like a wedding car trailing a string of cans.

Branding

It's an early morning in late spring, damp and foggy. Margaret MacKichan and I are going to photograph a branding. My contribution will be to wrestle calves while Margaret takes pictures. The ranch where we're going is a few miles south from the place my father and I own, along the road that runs across to Raven School.

I pick up Margaret at Mike and Dew Shonsey's in Long Pine—not much conversation at this hour—and we head south. It's hard to tell if the sun is up yet; it's light enough to drive without the headlights, but I leave them on for the patches of fog. There are puddles on the asphalt, and when I reach the end of the black-top, the gravel road is slippery on the surface. Nothing serious, but if it rains again the branding will have to be called off. You can't brand a wet calf; the moisture spreads out the heat of the iron so that all you get is a blotch.

Margaret's been over this road a couple of times, and she already has plenty of landscapes. Her cameras are in the bag, but she's looking around. The grass is mostly last year's, bleached pale by this time, but there's a fur of new growth underneath. Hardly enough to support cattle yet. Droplets of moisture cling to the fences, and every little pond along the road floats a pair of ducks. Mist-shapes balloon downward from the low cloud, nearly touching the road, but it

seems that the fog is lifting; I switch off the lights. I wish she would ask me to stop for her to take a photograph, but connubial ducks and foggy wisps and sparkling raindrops on last year's grass fail to interest her. From the beginning, the two of us have had different views of this project, and this morning the silence in the car is thick with that difference.

Past the fork we call "the Y," where the grade's built up to pass over a slough, a pair of mallards are out for their morning stroll. As I approach they hurry it up a little, but they're walking straight down the track, not across; I have to brake for them. "Out of the road, goofy ducks," I say under my breath. Two miles an hour, that's how fast a duck goes.

"The light's not right this morning," Margaret says. "I'm not going to get much contrast."

"Maybe they'll call it off," I say. "It's pretty wet."

"No they won't," she says. "The rain's stopped, don't you think?"

"I don't know." I wouldn't mind if they did call it off, since I'll be down on my butt in the muddy corral; Margaret's on a tight schedule, though, and this weekend and the next are all she has. "There's no telling if it'll rain again or not," I say. "If it does rain, they might work the calves out of a shed."

"I can't photograph in a shed," she says. Which isn't strictly true; if we have to work in a shed, she'll photograph in a shed, and her pictures will be wonderful. That isn't what she has in mind this morning. Barring rain, they'll be working the cattle on horseback; Margaret loves horses, and she favors that view of the ranch life. I've done my ranching from a tractor or a pickup truck, and I think she's got plenty of pictures of horses. But it's like my Aunt Myra telling Uncle Oz he had enough damned horses; I'd just as well keep shut about it.

"God's country," I say as we cross the autogate onto the Ross property. "Notice how much better the grass looks on this side of the fence."

"How far is it from your place to where we're going?"

"I don't know exactly," I tell her. "About four miles, I guess. There's the Edwards place, the old Fletcher place, and one in between that nobody's lived on since I can remember."

"Does anyone live at any of those?"

"Not that I know of," I say. "Not for a few years, anyway. The Barta brothers own the Edwards place, and Kenny Dillon had Fletcher's for a while. I don't know if the other one's even got buildings."

"What happens to these little places, then? Do the new owners keep them up?"

"It costs too much to maintain these old houses," I tell her. "Sometimes they keep the corrals fixed up, maybe a shed to park a tractor in."

"Hmp," she says. "In Lincoln you can't even find an apartment."

"I see what you're thinking," I say. "It does seem like a waste."

"I heard about a man in Los Angeles that has a used house lot," she says. "He buys houses that have to be moved and puts them on his lot, and people come and look at them and pick out the one they want. Couldn't you do something like that with these? Maybe low-income people could afford them."

"I suppose it's possible," I say. "But don't look at *me*."

We cross more autogates, passing the places in question. A branch of the road leads west, winding out of sight among grazed-off knolls, and I take it. Soon we come to a large windbreak and a cheerful set of buildings; the road goes through the yard. I look around but don't see any pickup trucks, any cattle, any sign of a branding.

"This is the place," I say. "Where is everybody?"

"Maybe they did call it off," she says.

"Maybe I've got the wrong day or something. But I was pretty sure." I feel like a klutz; I should've telephoned this morning. I hate to think I've dragged her all the way out here for nothing. I roll the window down, to listen if I can hear cattle bawling.

"Why don't you knock on the door," she says. "I don't think that dog'll bite you." A blue-heeler pup is lying by the garage, watching us but not barking. He looks as if he's recently been scolded.

A young woman, high-school age, answers the door. Yes, she says, they're branding in one of the pastures, over east. She points me in the right direction, shows me where the gate is. I go back out to the car, relieved.

"Got it right after all," I tell Margaret. "I guess they've already started. One of the girls is keeping an eye on dinner. God, the kitchen smells wonderful."

We pull on through the yard and turn through one of the pasture gates, heading more or less back the way we came. Once we're away from the buildings, I can hear the cows putting up a ruckus because their calves are sorted off. I drive confidently toward the noise, over a couple of hills, and come upon a cluster of vehicles around a yellow portable corral. Two ropers are already heeling calves, and smoke rises near the branding stove. Beside me, Margaret is swiftly organizing her equipment; I find a place to park and shut off the engine. Suddenly I'm the only one in sight who isn't doing something. I get out, close the door quietly, walk cautiously over to the corral, and watch for a minute or two, nodding as people look up from their work. Faces I haven't seen in a while slowly become familiar; I can put names to several of them, but there are too many I can't.

Margaret comes up and we go in together. Roger Brede, whose branding this is, is carrying a bloody jackknife and a can of Lysol, and when I introduce Margaret he doesn't offer to shake hands. I ask for my own assignment, hoping for something like vaccinating, not too hard on the knees, but he nods me in the direction of the ropers. The corral is divided into two parts, with a gate in between; as each calf is dragged backward through the gate, it gets pounced on by a pair of wrestlers, "thrown," and sat on while it is branded, dehorned (also with a hot iron), castrated if male, vaccinated, and ear-tagged. I catch the eye of another fellow who looks like he's between jobs, and the two of us grab the next one out. Since he's about half my age, I claim the shoulder to kneel on and let him sit on the ground.

The morning goes by quickly. Once in a while I look up and see Margaret dodging through the smoke, but mostly I'm occupied, collecting my share of strains and bruises. It's not unpleasant work, though, having as it does an element of play and chance. I'm not saying it's fun for the terrified calves.

No defense of hot-iron branding would convince an animal-rights activist. Freeze-branding, using a copper-alloy "iron" chilled in a slush of dry ice and methyl alcohol, seems less painful and makes a clearer mark; an alternative to branding, tattooing of the ear or lip, is already used to identify purebred livestock. Dehorning is unnecessary in that there are polled or "muley" versions of most breeds of cattle. As for castration, evidence that steers gain weight in the feedlot more quickly than bulls do has yet to come in. If preventing second-rate cattle from impregnating females is the point, a technique called "short-scrotuming" has been developed whereby the testicles are merely raised so that body heat prevents them from producing sperm.

(There are objections to these kinder techniques. An ear tattoo, for instance, is easily disposed of: the ear can simply be cut off. An animal must be caught for its tattoo to be read. A freeze-brand takes five minutes and forty cents' worth of dry ice per calf, besides the considerable initial cost of the irons. Short-scrotumed bulls, not to put too fine a point on it, behave like teen-agers. And polled cattle . . . well, some people just think they're ugly.)

From a practical standpoint, social brandings take up time in the spring when a lot of other work demands attention. For six weeks or so, a rancher can spend every Saturday and Sunday branding other people's cattle just so he can get some help with his own. All that rounding up and sorting off and stress and confusion doesn't do the cattle any good. And, once in a while a big steer calf will bleed to death after being dehorned, or will develop blood poisoning from a bad castration.

Why do it, then? Nickels and dimes add up when it's time to take calves to the sale barn. Young bulls "ought to" bring as much as steers, and calves with white freeze-brands on their sides "ought to" sell as high as any; but an auction contains as much psychology as a poker game, and "ought to" doesn't always apply in the sale ring. Five cents less per pound on a four-hundred-pound calf is minus twenty dollars; on a penful of a hundred calves that's a couple of thousand, and on four hundred calves it's enough to trade in (or, rather, *not* trade in) that clunker of a pickup on a shiny new four-wheel drive. In a thin year, a nickel a pound at auction time might mean the difference between paying something on your note at the bank, or borrowing money to pay the interest.

It's a week later. Another portable corral—more likely, the same one—has been set up on a different ranch, not many miles from where we were a week ago. Many of the same people are here, and it's even the same kind of weather: damp, threatening rain. My calf-wrestling partner is the son of a man I went to high school with. A big, good-looking fellow, he flirts hard with the young woman who comes around to put in ear tags. She doesn't pay him much attention, has seen a cowboy or two before. Other women are busy here. A short, dark-haired college girl is doing some of the heelroping today, and a woman in her fifties with an outdoor face is switching off handily between branding and vaccinating. It's always been that way, as far as I can tell; photographs dating back to the 1880s show women working cattle alongside the men. Girls whose families owned ranches, who grew up doing what they wanted to do, often chose work on the range and in the corrals over work in the kitchen. Some women did both, and some whose men were absent or debilitated did everything.

Margaret wants pictures of these women, but she's not having much luck getting their permission. They feel at a disadvantage, doing work that's smoky and dirty, their hair blown any old way. The men, too, behave oddly when the camera is pointed at them, clowning or posing, sometimes turning away. It helps that she's not the only photographer here; Clara Smith, married to our present host, is taking some snapshots. Last week, at the Brede place, Roger's dad was there with one of his eighty-year-old cronies, who was toting a video camera.

Last week we all said grace before lunch; this week, a bottle of Jim Beam is going around. Neighbors who can tolerate both prayer and whiskey have come to both brandings; those with an aversion to one or the other can opt out freely enough. Sandhills people aren't all alike by any means, and when it's time to share work, broad differences are put up with. But not everyone has the same set of friends, so every crew is a little different. Maybe half the people here today were at the Brede place a week ago.

Some of the men are roasting calves' nuts on the branding stove; I am offered one. I chew it up, not hiding my distaste. It's gristly and tastes like you'd expect: charcoal flavored with a little urine.

"Needs mustard," I say.

The food inside the house is a lot better. Clara runs the Depot, one of Ainsworth's cafés, and she's used to putting out good food in large quantities. The young man who happens to sit by me is a Micheel, another son of someone I knew in school. I get him into a con-versation about Doc Micheel, a cowboy of my father's generation, this boy's granddad's brother. I hear things I never knew before, family stories about different times Doc got himself hurt and had to be sewn up. Mary, the older woman so adept in the corral, is sitting on the other side of him and chimes in with stories of her own, and I learn a dozen fascinating incidents that I'll forget the details of by the time I get to a typewriter. Mary knows George Anderson, one of the oldest cowboys still living in the area, and I mention that I'd like to get George talking into a tape recorder. Mary tells me it won't work; she says he has a daughter who's been trying it for years.

As the two of us are leaving, it starts to rain, a light sprinkle that may not last. The men have a pitch game going in one of the sheds; as we pass by, one of them stops us to ask Margaret an off-color riddle. There's a few head left to brand, fall calves that got sorted off from the main bunch, and enough of the crew is staying to take care of them. Margaret's got her negatives, I've got my lumps. We won't be missed.

Instead of going back to Ainsworth, I take the Elsmere Road past Willow Lake and into the Goose Creek country. Passing one pond we see cormorants. The road winds its way among wet meadows that are greening up, and forks and forks again; I miss a turn or two. Finally, I find a mail route and follow it north, hoping it'll take us into Johnstown. (We end up in

Wood Lake instead, ten miles further west.) Because I'm lost, the country all looks the same to me, and I apologize to Margaret for boring her with it.

"Takes a lot to bore me," she says.

The thing that struck her most about the two brandings was how patient people were with one another. No one really gave orders, no one yelled at anybody; when someone standing in the wrong place and looking the wrong way held things up a bit, whoever he was in the way of just stopped and waited for him to wake up. Children were a nuisance, in and out of the corrals all morning, but none got shouted at or spanked. Other places she's been, other people she's photographed wouldn't have been like that, she says.

I don't know what to make of this, not having heard it before. Maybe it's because the work is dangerous, I tell her; patience is important because the potential for an accident is always there. As for the kids, the corral is still the only school for this business; maybe people are just glad they're interested. But these explanations sound hollow, like something made up to fill a gap in the conversation.

The truth is that there's something going on at a branding that I don't fully understand with my mind, though maybe I recognize it in my heart. Amid that strange violence is a curious streak of gentleness and good will, mixed with nostalgia. The old-timers had a saying that it was a tough country for women and horses, but great for men and mules. Meaning, I suppose, that it took a certain mulishness to ride out the ups and downs of the cattle business. Times have changed and mules are gone from the sandhills, but the economic ride is as bumpy as ever. If I had to make up a saying now, I'd call it a terrific country for cattle, but hard on ranchers. Those men we left joking and playing pitch don't know which of them, with their families, will be gone from the table at branding time next year.

There's a delight in doing a thing the way you learned it, not in school where the teacher can be the bearer of so much bad news, but beside your father and uncles in the dust of the corral. Maybe that's why you'll occasionally see some middle-aged guy who obviously belongs in town, out of breath and rubbing his bruises, getting up slowly and a little bit in the way, wrestling calves beside the youngsters in the smoke of the branding irons.

1 *Road to Ravenscroft*, Cherry County, January 1979

2 *Roundup on McGrew's 700*, Custer County, June 1977

3 *Herding, Broken Box Ranch,* October 1989

4 *Ropers, McGrew's 700*, Custer County, June 1977

5 *John Slagle*, Custer County, June 1977

6 *Saddling Foxy Lady,* Cherry County, May 1979

7 *On the Rim of the Loup,* Blaine County, June 1977

8 *Carla Henderson*, Box Butte County, June 1979

9 *Separated Cattle*, Thomas County, October 1978

10 *Waiting Behind*, Merriman Rodeo, October 1989

11 *Joy Lue Moreland*, Merriman, September 1979

12 *Stan and Bob*, Cherry County, May 1979

13 *Ropers, Green Valley,* Cherry County, May 1990

14 *Before Branding, Green Valley*, Cherry County, May 1979

15 *Branding, Roger Brede's,* Brown County, May 1989

16 *Young Observer*, Cherry County, May 1991

17 *Dan Dailey on Paint*, Cherry County, May 1991

18 *Sorting Cattle, Broken Box Ranch*, Cherry County, October 1989

19 *Starting Young*, Cherry County, May 1979

20 *Branding, John Smith's,* Brown County, May 1989

21 *After Branding, Green Valley,* Cherry County, May 1979

22 *Niomia McGrew,* Custer County, September 1979

23 *Sandhills Road*, Custer County, June 1977

24 *Riders*, Blaine County, June 1977

25 *Carol Moreland,* Cherry County, September 1979

26 *May,* Cherry County, 1989

27 *Bill Henderson,* Box Butte County, June 1979

28 *Along the Snake,* Cherry County, September 1979

29 *Raye Jean and Chad*, Custer County, September 1979

30 *Frank Hardy,* Cherry County, October 1978

31 *Brad Adamson, Broken Box Ranch*, Cherry County, October 1989

32 *Ken Moreland,* Cherry County, October 1989

33 *Cooksley Corral*, Custer County, June 1977

34 *Overlooking the Ranch*, Cherry County, June 1977

35 *Calf in the Cradle*, Custer County, June 1977

36 *Ed Sherbeck, Taking a Break,* Custer County, June 1977

37 *Branding and Dehorning*, Custer County, June 1977

38 *Ready to Load 'em*, Custer County, September 1979

39 *Making Hay with the Slide Stacker,* Cherry County, September 1979

40 *Billy Jo Cornish, Hired Hand,* Cherry County, March 1985

41 *Old-Timer's Rodeo, Hyannis,* Grant County, September 1979

42 *Tack*, Custer County, June 1977

43 *At the Sale*, Thomas County, October 1978

44 *Brand Inspector, Thedford,* Thomas County, October 1978

45 *Spearhead Ranch,* Cherry County, March 1985

46 *Thedford Sale Barn*, Thomas County, October 1978

47 *October Storm*, Cherry County, October 1978

48 *Paul Krajeski, Coyote Hunter*, Cherry County, January 1979

49 *Don McGuire, Muley-Making,* Cherry County, March 1979

50 *Glen Corbin,* Thomas County, October 1978

51 *Tammy Turner*, Cherry County, February 1979

52 *Mr. Turner*, Cherry County, February 1979

53 *Jody Lovejoy*, Cherry County, March 1979

54 *Midwinter*, Cherry County, January 1979

55 *Chores*, Cherry County, March 1979

56 *John Johnson, Breaking Ice*, Cherry County, January 1979

57 *Winterscape*, Cherry County, 1982

58 *Buck Buckles Feeding with Percherons,* Cherry County, January 1979

59 *Snowscape*, Cherry County, March 1979

60 *Nancy Jean Moreland*, Cherry County, May 1979

61 *Winter*, Cherry County, February 1982

62 *Tiff Moreland*, Cherry County, May 1990

63 *January—Bulls at Minus 20,* Cherry County, January 1979

64 *Newborn at Lawrence Turner's,* Cherry County, February 1979

65 *May Blizzard*, Cherry County, May 1979

Boys

A vital part of my education began when, after firing Joe Carlsen for the second time, Dad decided that he and his brother Ozro could operate on shares; Oz's place south of Ainsworth and our ranch south of Long Pine were just three miles apart as the crow flies. Uncle Oz agreed, and I and an orange Allis-Chalmers tractor went over as part of the deal. I was tall and tender at thirteen; my bald-headed, roughneck uncle would've been fifty-three.

Though I'd done ranch work previously, I was in most respects a typical small-town kid. My summers had been devoted to reading, Boy Scouts, Little League baseball, and just plain goofing around with friends; I had of course been asked, ordered, bribed, and cajoled to mow the lawn and do a few other household chores, but I was adept at avoiding most kinds of work, and mostly I got away with it. What I did best was read; I spent hours alone with books. Maybe my parents figured that as long as I was improving my mind, it didn't matter if I didn't do much for their property values. Suddenly, however, all this summertime comfort came to an end, for I had been traded.

For maybe ten years before that, Oz had put up hay on contract for some big ranches in the Timber Lake country, over in South Dakota. He would round up a crew out of the Longhorn, the Silver Circle, and a few similar establishments, trail his machinery north, and spend a hot, glorious summer as a minor king of the hayfields. He was a shrewd and hearty boss who kept his employees impressed by outworking them during the week and outwitting them on the weekends, so that in spite of their best efforts they ended up back in camp on Monday morning. Oz loved that country; his wife, Myra, said later that she thought he might have relocated there, but "I wouldn't live in a place where rattlesnakes came right up in the yard." Contract haying suited Oz, but it was ultimately not very profitable, and I think Myra, weary of cooking for so many under such conditions and dizzy with watching the money come and go, put her foot down and made him give it up. However that was, Aunt Myra's nephew E. B. and I were to be the main part of Oz's hay crew for the next four years.

The first thing we learned was getting up in the morning. Each day at six a.m., Oz stepped off the screen porch and bawled us up out of bed in the same note he used for calling his cows. E. B. and I slept in an old schoolhouse that Oz had bought for next to nothing and moved onto the place. It sat a good hundred yards from the house, but we could hear him plain, and if we didn't respond pretty rapidly he would oblige us by coming closer and hollering louder. Our first task after washing ("Always wash first thing in the morning, boys, you don't know where those hands have been") was to buckle down to Aunt Myra's breakfast, which was milk, eggs, sausage or bacon, and all the thin oblong pancakes a teen-age boy could eat.

At breakfast we would have to endure E. B.'s three younger sisters. In the absence of adults, these three imps were held in check by their brother's established tyranny, but in the freedom of the breakfast table they were a lively trio of teasers, and their favorite target was me. As the bookish child of parents who were ten years older than the parents of most of my friends, I had never gotten much teasing. I blushed easily, defenseless, and the three of them knew no mercy.

Oz hoped to bring in money by using his best ground more intensively—by turning part of his ranch into a farm. This required irrigation; the system he chose used aluminum sprinkler pipe that had to be hand-carried. Twice each day, we disassembled a quarter-mile of four-inch pipe into thirty-foot sections and moved it forty feet across the fields. To use the corn and alfalfa he grew, Oz bought dairy cows, so morning and evening our chores were the same: milking cows and carrying pipe.

Between chores and chores, what we boys did varied as the summer moved along. As hay hands, we started out running mowers, so each of us was responsible for his own small tractor and mowing machine. During the first part of the summer these required a lot of maintenance, to be put in shape for the main haying season that began after the Fourth of July. Later, there was the haying itself. Oz would hire an older fellow for the haying season, or, after E. B. and I became a year or two older, a third boy. Although we worked as a crew, mowing is rather solitary by nature, especially in a large pasture; the tractors travel at slightly different speeds, and are subject to various accidents and brief stoppages. When you begin cutting a 320-acre pasture, it takes over an hour to make the first round, and once the mowers become scattered along the perimeter, each driver more or less has the morning to himself, out of sight among the soft swells of the hills.

Once the grass was cut and raked into windrows, the stacking operation that followed required much more teamwork. Oz drove the "sweep," a John Deere Model A tractor that had a turned-around seat and was run in reverse. The sweep "buck" was a tractor-wide comb with twelve-foot hickory teeth, used to gather loose hay from the windrows and bring it to the stacker. We used a slide stacker: another buck similar to the one on the back of the sweep tractor carried the hay up a wooden ramp and dropped it onto the stack. Power to raise the stacker buck came from one of the mower tractors, pulling a heavy rope that ran through pulleys out the side of the stacker.

In addition to the sweep (which, minus the sweep buck and running in the proper direction, was Oz's main farming tractor) and the three mowers, there was a little John Deere Model H that carried the three-rake hitch. This was not much more than a channel-iron that bolted across the front, to which were tied three fourteen-foot rakes. The rakes were tripped with a lever arrangement that required a constantly active arm; this outfit moved fast and rode rough, and it was the one rig you never saw an adult driving.

Though I didn't realize it at the time, our way of haying had been brought straight over from the horse technology my father and uncles grew up with. In particular, the slide stacker was a wooden-framed machine designed originally to be worked by horses; the three-rake hitch was mounted on a tractor, but each individual high-wheeled rake still carried an iron seat on which the driver of a team might have ridden. Our mowers, though made for tractors, had certain parts that would interchange with the old horse-drawn ones. The sweep, too, had a horse-powered predecessor, pushed rather than pulled by a team of four. If Oz had stepped from his own boyhood over a hill and into a hayfield of the late fifties, he would've been surprised at the proliferation of tractors, but he would not have been puzzled by any of the tasks.

The adage "Make hay while the sun shines" refers to what anyone who has a lawn to mow knows if he or she thinks about it, that you can't make any hay when it's raining. Anytime it rained, there were always plenty of other jobs to do, like sharpening and riveting sickles. Also, wherever you have feed and animals to consume it, you have manure. Therefore, another job that was pretty regular for us in spring and early sum-

mer was hauling the cleanings from the horse and dairy barns onto the sandy patches out in the fields. Part of it was back-bending physical work but not as ugly as one might think; we had a hydraulic loader and a mechanical spreader, and there was a clear benefit in that the manure helped to keep the June wind from sandblasting the young corn.

Oz kept a stud and a half-dozen quarter-horse mares at a time when there wasn't much demand for little colts and fillies. Often in June our day of pounding rivets would be interrupted by a pickup truck with a horse trailer bouncing into the yard, with a mare neighing in the back and answering squeals coming from the direction of the barn. Some business for Poco Revenue. E. B. and I would tag along to watch. I don't know that viewing horse sex should be part of every boy's experience, but it was part of ours; if the whole business was edifying, it was only so in that one saw that sex is a heavy-duty force in the world, and a person still slight and unsure of his footwork might do well to keep out of its way.

Our uncle was a fine boss to work for, boyish himself in some important way, and those summers passed swiftly. And there were days when Oz would look around in the middle of a hot afternoon, cock his grizzled eyebrows at us, and say, "Why don't you boys take the pickup over to Hagan Lake and catch some bass?" Along with our labor we had a little independence; most city boys in their early teens don't have the opportunity to take a truck several miles, go out in a rowboat, and spend a day fishing or loafing, or discussing their uncle's character, as they choose.

E. B. and I treated Oz and Myra's place as our own, even borrowing their car to go into town once we were old enough to drive legally; we read freely from a huge pile of paperbacks in the attic, some of which were clearly written for young people like ourselves, though the illustrations showed they were from an earlier generation. There were other things up there, old toys, child-sized clothing, sheepskin jackets; they were worn-out mostly, shabby, not very interesting. I don't remember giving them a thought. The books were odd; Edgar Rice Burroughs's stories about the planet Barzoom were among them, and a short thick adventure whose leading character was Little Orphan Annie. There were even tiny books whose pages each contained one drawing of a single figure; if you riffled the pages quickly under your thumb, the figure appeared to move. We read them all because we needed something to pass the time in the evenings, and didn't worry about who they might have belonged to. In fact, they belonged to a previous family of boys, and those boys were Oz's.

Aunt Myra was Uncle Oz's second wife. They got married in 1949, when Oz was forty-five; Myra would've been in her late thirties. I don't know whether Myra hoped for children, but no children

came. Maybe that's why she took summertime care of other people's. Besides E. B. and me, and E. B.'s three sisters, there was usually another boy from town hired during the haying season, and I had city cousins who came every year, three girls from the suburbs of Chicago. Some weeks the house and bunkhouse filled up and overflowed into the yard. Oz's three sons had children of their own, and often a scattering of them would stay a while, too.

When Oz married his first wife, Velma Cate, in March of 1927, he was twenty-two; she was not quite eighteen. Velma was soon pregnant, and before long the young couple had three sons, Darald, Louie, and Ernie. They lived near Clearfield, South Dakota, just about twenty miles north of Johnstown; Oz went into various ventures in partnership with his father-in-law, W. B. "Red" Cate, but the older man, though a capable worker, was a disastrous gambler, and they did not prosper. When grasshoppers took over Tripp County in 1934, the young couple moved back to the sandhills, living on Willow Lake and Hagan Lake before settling near the Beardwell post office on the Calamus River. Over the winter of 1938–39, Oz had a bit of luck, trapping enough muskrats to pay for a new car; in September of 1939, Velma Ross died of pneumonia. Darald was eleven, Louie eight, and Ernie Ross was six years old.

Between September of 1939 and October of 1949, when he married Myra, Oz raised his boys more or less alone, sometimes with the help of his mother-in-law, "Red" Cate's wife. They moved to the ranch we knew later as Oz and Myra's. The "Dirty Thirties" were over, and they worked and held onto the place, but maybe they missed some gentleness in their lives. Oz was the kind of Dutch uncle every teen-age boy needs; E. B. and I benefited enormously by his teaching and example. At the same time, we could go home on the weekends, and for nine months of the year we led a town life, focused on school. Oz and Velma's boys had a different kind of experience; these older cousins whom I hardly knew, whom we saw only as visitors, were the true heirs of the place. It's worth noting that, once they were on their own, none of them chose to make a life in the sandhills.

When Dad and Oz together leased a third ranch, the Edwards place, Oz had to buy some stock cows to use his share of the grass. Somehow he got hold of a bunch of open-range cattle from a reservation up in Montana. These were good, hardy Hereford cows, very much able to look out for themselves and their calves, but they came off the cattle truck like ballerinas on speed, fleeing a burning theater.

One of "those Montana cows" that made our lives interesting for a while was a big, burly, curly yellow cow that had too much milk for a baby calf to handle. If she could be milked by hand for a couple of weeks, her calf would then be able to take all she could produce, and would grow to be one of the biggest calves

in the herd. But that "if" was a pretty big one. The job, of course, fell to E. B. and me. We kept a horse at my parents' ranch (no humans lived there at the time) and would drive over once a day to get this old cow in and milk her out.

E. B. did the cowboying; as he brought her through the pens, it was my job to close the gates behind them, hemming horse, rider, and cow into smaller and smaller enclosures until the cow was in the corral. From there we got her into the barn, then into a series of stalls that led finally to a chute, where we caught her in a headstall, put an iron bar through the boards behind her, tied one of her hind feet back, and milked her. That was the theory, anyway; the cow had other ideas. For one thing, she was boss cow of the herd, not much used to putting up with nonsense, and she saw no reason to be afraid of a couple of puny two-legged creatures such as we were. She respected a man on horseback, but a boy on foot in a corral was another matter. Also, she had no love of corrals and chutes. We had gotten her in once to work on her teeth (she gave every indication of wanting to work on *our* teeth) and she hadn't forgotten the experience. Last but not least, her udder was sore. So each day we had to outwit her in a slightly different manner, with a thoughtful eye to not getting ourselves killed.

One day when E. B. brought her into the east pen, I showed myself too early and she went out through the barbedwire fence. E. B. opened the gate again (you can't take a horse through a busted wire fence) and went after her, putting her in the west pen this time. She took a look at the corral gate, ran back past the horse, and went through another fence into a stackyard. E. B. opened the stackyard gate and went in to get her, whereupon she went through the stackyard fence in a new place, ignoring both the gate and the hole she had made previously, and out into the holding pasture where her calf was. Not satisfied, she kept on going, right through the holding pasture fence and out where the rest of the cattle were.

E. B. was disgusted, the horse was tired, and we now had four torn-up fences to fix. We went home and told Oz that the cow had turned herself out, and that we weren't going to milk her any more. It was the one time I can remember that we ever mutinied.

The last summer I worked for Uncle Oz, another uncle, Frank Behr of Norfolk, came up to join us on the hay crew.

Of all the relatives, Uncle Frank was Oz's favorite companion. A barrel-chested little man with a deep voice and snapping gray eyes, Frank Behr was chief brand inspector for the Norfolk sale barn, so that every head of livestock sold there had to pass under his gaze; in that capacity he was a bureaucrat by profession, albeit a horseback one. Like Oz, however, he had been a young practitioner of the cowboy life. Frank ran away from home at the age of fifteen, first finding

work at the Hanna ranch deep in Cherry County, where he learned to rope and to handle a team. He took to ranch life, becoming a skilled hand at whatever needed doing, until he met Alberta Ross, Oz's youngest sister, who had come into that remote country to teach school. Once they married, there was a need for money, and money was one satisfaction that a ranch job did not provide. Frank tried selling cars for a while, then got on as brand inspector at Grand Island, finally moving to Norfolk around 1960.

Whenever Frank and Oz got together, they were apt to have a bit of extracurricular fun. The summer before, Frank had come up for a two-week visit, and he and Oz had impressed the neighbors by driving Frank's Volkswagen across the east end of Willow Lake. This summer, though, Frank had come to work. He moved into the high-windowed old schoolhouse where E. B. and I slept and made up a bunk alongside ours.

Two things about Frank bothered us that summer. The first was that, except for short naps in the hayfield following lunch, he apparently never slept. Each of us reported waking in pitch blackness to see the red glow of his cigarette. Frank had asthma and packed a powerful snore, so his not sleeping might have been merely considerate. Still.

The other thing was that he acted like a boy. Frank was over fifty, yet he insisted on riding in the back of the pickup, competing with us to open gates. One time I was riding shotgun in the passenger's side of the cab when we came to a gate; thinking it was my turn, I opened the door just as Frank jumped down from the box. He hit the door solid and it knocked him spinning. He laughed to show that it hadn't hurt, but E. B. and I were more careful of him after that.

Frank was a capable, active man, but he wasn't used to our way of doing things, and E. B. and I couldn't boss him the way we could our peers from town. He seized on hard and humble jobs, but running the scatter-rake was too rough for him (as it would've been for anyone who didn't have a rubber spine) and working on top of the haystack bothered his asthma. Mowing, the best and easiest hayfield job, is unutterably and abysmally boring to some people; Uncle Oz hated it with a passion, and Frank's disposition was similar.

That year, Oz had traded in his slowpoke GMC for a glossy burgundy Chevy pickup that had better highway speed. One late morning after a particularly heavy rain, we were crossing a neighbor's pasture on our way to Hagan Lake, where Oz hadn't been able to resist taking on a hay contract. It had been wet all summer, with plenty of interruptions to the haying, and the track across that section of land had become a maze, winding along the ridges between potholes and sloughs. Oz and Frank had their heads together in the cab, and when they glanced back at us and grinned, E. B. and I crouched lower in the box. A standard joke was for the driver to "accidentally" blunder through hubcap-deep water, cooling off the riders in back.

When Oz topped the next ridge, we caught our breath. He'd picked a pothole two-and-a-half feet deep. There was a terrific splash, and an icy sheet of water poured up and over the cab, drenching us. As the truck coughed to a stop on the other side, we heard a metallic scraping sound from the engine compartment. Pink cheeks shiny, still smothering a giggle, Oz got out and raised the hood. Along with pond water and sand, bright-green antifreeze dribbled into the grass; the wet impact had shoved the radiator back into the fan. As Oz's muscular neck got redder and redder, all Frank could do was wink at us; radiators cost too much to be funny, and we were all four going to have to walk.

Oz gave Frank a young mare as part of his wages. She was a pretty thing, with buckskin markings like Rev's; Frank spent his evenings and weekends gentling her. Toward the end of summer, he took a notion that he ought to hurry her along. Oz disagreed; it wasn't his way of breaking horses. But she was Frank's mare by then.

One gray Sunday, while Oz was checking pastures and we boys were in town, Aunt Myra was at the sink, peeling potatoes for dinner, when she heard a commotion and glanced out the window. Down by the horse barn there was an eight-foot windbreak, so she couldn't see the corral; what she did see was a horse's back and Uncle Frank rising high above the boards. The second time she saw horsehide there was nothing sticking up but the saddle horn, so she dried her hands and started down there. He was on his feet when she got to him, hugging a corral plank and wheezing. When I saw him Monday morning, he was sitting stiffly upright and sipping at his cigarette like a man held together with tape, waiting for Alberta to come up from Norfolk and take him home.

Dad and Oz got along OK as brothers, but as business partners they inevitably had their differences. Their partnership came to an end when Dad found a couple to live on the place, about the time that I went off to college. After that, when I came home for the summer I worked for Dad directly.

For a number of years, my Uncle Oz was the man in the world whom I admired most. He chewed me out for my many failures of concentration, but my most painful failing—a lack of that manly fearlessness Oz himself had in abundance—he treated with gentleness and tact. He did me the honor of never asking me to be a different boy than I was.

At the same time, there were tensions. Oz had a way of irritating my mother by calling her "schoolmom." His greeting for me was a booming "Howdy, String-bean!" accompanied by a crushing grip on my upper arm, mashing my biceps under his thumb. There came a time when this got wearisome, especially as it grew clearer that the kind of life I was aiming for was not one which would ever build much muscle.

After the Vietnam issue polarized the country, there were years when my uncle and I could barely talk to one another. When I came home to live by myself on the ranch, our relationship improved, but I never again regarded this unrepentant George Wallace Democrat as my personal model. He was a man of fixed ideas, some of which were repugnant to me. I also became more aware of another side of him. Because I'd developed a taste for alcohol, I could now recognize in my uncle a man who drank. Ultimately, this did not change my respect for him, but it explained some things.

I got together with Oz and Frank again, one last time. Frank and Alberta had come to Ainsworth for a weekend, and the three older couples—Oz and Myra, Frank and Bertie, and my parents—decided to go fishing. I went along. We drove south from Ainsworth to Willow Lake, taking two cars and one twelve-foot boat; the plan was to take turns, some fishing from the bank while others used the boat. I, the responsible one, was sent out with my two old-boy uncles, supposedly in charge of the outboard motor. Our lines were hardly damp when Frank produced a pint of Wild Turkey, and, like a colt eating peppermints, I was quickly led astray. The three of us had a fine turkey-calling contest out there on the lake, and watched the sun go down in bourbon-colored splendor, while the folks on shore fought mosquitoes and the wise perch nibbled away our baits.

Frank had himself a stroke not long after that. We all drove down to Norfolk, to see him staring in silent terror at the somber relatives filing past his bed. A week later, he had the final one. Though I was back living on my folks' place by then, I hadn't yet got around to selling the VW bus I'd bought in Tucson. It had a bad axle bearing, but I drove it to town anyway because days of steady rain had soaked the road, and it was the only vehicle I had that would plow through the thirteen miles of mud between our ranch and the nearest asphalt.

It had rained in Norfolk too, so that the clay soil at the cemetery was saturated, and when we had shuffled and prayed and had turned our backs to go, the line of cars pulling away from the grave started to get stuck. I and my cousin's husband, the youngest adults, got out in our best suits and started pushing cars. We were ankle-deep in red-brown muck, and the spinning tires sprayed us with cold slime the texture of cow manure. It was the kind of thing where you either have to laugh or curse, and because it was a funeral, we laughed. A dinner at the Methodist church followed the funeral; I remember wiping clay off my shoes in the basement of the fellowship hall, thinking that if Frank had been there he'd have had a little something to warm us up, Methodists or no Methodists.

The last time I talked to Oz was in the spring of 1990. I had gone to the coffee shop to meet my father; we were sitting with another older fellow when Oz came in. He'd been having trouble with one of his feet, a sore deep in his instep that wouldn't heal, and we

were worried about him. Oz was eighty-six, had diabetes, and the doctors were threatening to take his leg off. Dad and Oz and the third man got to talking about their health problems, and the conversation was not a cheerful one. I'd been working on my house and wanted to get back to it, so I said, "You're about a gloomy bunch. Before you old farts depress me, I think I'll go home and drive some nails."

Oz's cheeks turned pink, and he shot me a look from his merry old go-to-hell eyes. "Hop right to it, Stringbean," he boomed. "Time is wastin'." I laughed, got up, and left them there, three old men sipping coffee, tasting their memories.

On another long-ago fishing trip, Oz's boyhood pal Win Baldwin spurred his pony off the bank, carrying one end of a seine. The bank was over a deep hole, so that after they went in, all that was visible for a few seconds was Win's hat floating on the water. For me, that glance of Oz's was like Win's hat, the image I'll remember. My uncle was no ideal citizen, but a fine man in his way. Once upon a time he gave me some room to grow in, and showed me that a person can work hard and have some fun at the same time. He loved the earth he stood on, and he stood on it strongly, a stern-faced man with light-colored, laughing eyes. He kept fit well past his middle years, into his seventies, and was still oak-solid when we put him in the ground. I know; along with E. B., I was one of his pallbearers. His coffin was heavy.

The Lost City

Each December, a life-size manger scene is put up in front of our courthouse, along with a sign: "Welcome to Ainsworth, Christmas City of the Sandhills." After midnight, when the semis pull through on Highway 20, heaters turned up and tape players blasting out Farron Young, calm angels and shepherds watch them safely past. The drivers are mostly young, their lives ahead of them, and it's black ice on the curves, four long hours to Sioux City.

Better than angels and shepherds would be a hot cup of coffee. There used to be a 24-hour truck stop here, Masters' Nite-n'-Day, but it's been a while since it was open after 10 p.m. Now called the Hiway 20 Cafe, it caters to farmers mostly, contractors and mechanics, entrepreneurs of other than the downtown businesses. When a waitress unlocks the door at six o'clock, there'll be a couple of cars in the parking lot, engines running to keep the drivers warm. Old guys, probably, who got up to pee and didn't go back to bed. My father will be among them, the first ones out of the dark.

Now pairs of headlights swerve in off the highway, dip to a stop. Steam swirls at the door as the overshod men come in. In the kitchen, the cook has begun a sprint that will last through sunup into midmorning, and the waitresses hurry to get orders in and the hot plates served. Sausage, bacon, eggs, pancakes, waffles, French toast, toast and hashbrowns; once in a while an omelet, a few hot cereals. There are moist glazed rolls that weigh a quarter of a pound in a case by the register. You won't see a bagel or a slice of melon in the place. The plume from an idling diesel rises above the frozen parking lot; the eastern horizon is graying, frost at the bottom of a night-black window. A winter day begins.

At a ranch south of Long Pine, twenty miles from town, the horizon is elevated by a line of hills, so the sun has gathered most of its force by the time it sends long shadows across the meadow. A man hurries out of the house, rubbing his arms because he's not dressed for the weather, and stoops to connect the engine heater of his tractor to an extension cord that leads inside the wellhouse. Whinnying from the cold, he runs back inside, not stopping to notice how frost steams away from the purple grass-stems, how light suffuses the landscape like a vapor. These things can be witnessed from the warm kitchen, or could be; the window is not particularly clean.

The man is a writer. His morning's task—set by himself, since no one else seems interested—is to reflect on what he sees as a decline in the ethnic diversity and in the cultural aspirations of his community. There are a few bald facts to consider (he, too, is at his breakfast now, pancakes and bacon, same as if he lifted bales for a living). The county's population has declined steadily since 1940, and the average age of the present inhabitants is high. His problem is that, first of all, the few relevant statistics can't be expanded into a full-length essay, and second, that he has a *feeling*, which the facts don't satisfactorily reinforce. He is lonesome and miserable, and has nobody to talk to. This, he feels certain, must be Brown County's fault.

He gets up, places his plate in the sink (other dishes already occupy the sink; he will wash them when he runs out of clean forks, or a meal or two thereafter) and approaches his desk, carrying a cup of tea. The desk is solid, made of an old door and some concrete blocks, and the gray typewriter on it also looks as if it would stand some abuse. There are many papers, few of which have anything to do with his project. A small sheaf lies just beside the typewriter; he picks up the topmost sheet and, wrinkling his nose, reads:

Grace M. Weiss, former librarian at the Alder Public Library in Ainsworth, says in *Along Pioneer Trails* that "an unverified report states that Kate Litz was the earliest settler in Long Pine in 1876." If it's so, Kate was a couple of years or a wagon ride ahead of the end of track; the railroad arrived by 1880. By 1890, only a decade after real settlement began, the population of Brown County had already passed 4300. It passed 6000 after 1920, but has been declining since World War II; today there are less than there were in 1890. Outside the three towns, the decline has been dramatic.

The homesteaders and the Kincaiders who followed them were people of all types. All nations of northern Europe were represented; there were Yankees and southerners, and a few blacks. Probably the most common demographic category was unmarried adult males, but there were many families and remnants of families as well as single women. A surprising proportion were of middle age. . . .

Our author stands in a frowning reverie, visualizing sweet, earnest, roly-poly little Grace M. Weiss perched like a broody hen amid her dusty trove of books, pecking at the reaching hands of children. Mrs. Weiss, in fact, was a nice woman; but whenever this young sourball hears the word "nice," it conjures up a rusted fortress of things-as-we-blindly-hope-they-were, so that he believes it is the poet's duty as a lackey of Truth to be a lifelong enemy of niceness. Still, not being nice won't matter if he can't write better than this. Something reminds him that his bowels haven't yet moved. He puts down his teacup and retires in the direction of the bathroom.

By the time our scholar gets back to work, the library in Ainsworth—the new one, not the talcy, overheated dungeon of his imagination and memory—is just opening. The new library is a low, modern, handicapped-accessible brick building with a hip roof (the former librarian at the high school, where a flat roof had leaked and caused damage to the books, was on the fund-raising committee). There's plenty of light and air, and a minimum of dust. The collection is skimpy by urban standards, but a statewide network exists by which books can be quickly borrowed from other libraries. Even so, it holds three times as many books as could be fitted into the old building.

Besides the library, the courthouse block contains the courthouse (a modern building, built in 1959), the sheriff's office and jail (not so modern), and the Sellers Museum, which looks something like a homesteader's cabin in a Western movie but whose latest log wing was laid and chinked about ten years ago. There are trees, swings, and picnic tables, and just now, of course, the crèche. Everything looks in good repair. The block is partly a city park, but the main city park is located on the east side of town.

(Here is a list of things that used to be in the courthouse park that aren't there now: a peeling wooden bandstand, six- or eight-sided, with screen in its windows; a square cast-iron fountain and watering trough, ten or twelve feet on a side, whose fluted skirts were sprayed with aluminum paint; an ornate cast-iron drinking fountain shaped like a samovar, with a second bowl at ground level that would serve for dogs; and a few dozen eighty-year-old American elms. If the Dutch elm disease hadn't come through town, there would've been a fuss about putting the new library where it is.)

Main Street and Highway 20 form one corner of the block. Across the highway, all along the west side of Main Street, the sun is lighting up the fronts of buildings: a hotel, the post office, the old library (now a hair salon), some lawyers' offices, the newspaper office, the Nebraska Public Power District office, an optometrist's office, and a bank. Like the library, the bank has just opened; a man wearing dark-green coveralls and high-heeled overshoes waits on the mourners' bench, felt hat on his knee. Past the bank, past the Coast-to-Coast store and the optometrist's, the last building on the block is given over to social services. Unemployment in Brown County is low, but of those who work full-time a number remain poor, in particular single or divorced women and their children. The theme everywhere this time of year is Christmas, and the windows of this office are decorated with triangular paper trees, with hairy ropes of tinsel.

On around the corner, past the alley, the winter sun draws a warm bronze color from the tan brick of the United Methodist church. Of Ainsworth's ten churches, it's the one built closest to a bank. The minister, a gawky, good-hearted, rather shy fellow, is working up his Christmas sermon; though he loves the paradox of God as a helpless baby, he sometimes wishes the Three Wise Men had left their fancy presents at home.

Twenty-five miles southwest, on Enders Lake, the late fishermen are going out to fish, ice creepers strapped to their overshoes, their tip-ups loaded in boxes that are also sleds. They pass the early fishermen going home and exchange items of encrypted misinformation. The ice is nearly transparent, only four inches thick but strong enough to hold a truck; bubbles can be seen clearly against the black water below.

By eleven-thirty our lonely author has gotten busy at last. The keys of his typewriter clack forlornly as he describes the enlightened community he imagines his ancestors imagined would blossom at the edge of the sandhills. Poets, musicians, visual artists, actors and dancers they must've foreseen themselves engendering, he thinks, or, at the very least, liberal-minded citizens who wouldn't demand that he forswear communism and indecency before extending him aid in the form of a nice, fat, juicy NEA grant.

Outside, the sun is shining brightly, although high clouds seem to be moving in from the south. A yellow-and-white short-tailed dog lies curled against the stucco wall on the south side of the house, waiting for his master to finish up at the typewriter and come outdoors. The engine heater on the feeding tractor percolates cheerfully, and the cattle are beginning to gather along the fence. It would be a fine day, the dog thinks, for catching sparrows along the haystacks, if only there were a little snow. Oh well, he thinks, better to be bored than hungry, and closes his eyes to nap a while again.

In Ainsworth, the Senior Citizen's Center crowd is gathering for lunch. The Center is another relatively new brick building, and its constituency is a large and lively one; people who lived different kinds of lives during their working years and who hardly mixed at all socially now come together for lunch, five days a week. The atmosphere is cheery and skeptical. Folks in their sixties sit down with older folks in their nineties, and the generation's worth of age difference seems less important than it used to. Conversation deals mostly with local events and with the health of friends, for this is a group conscious of living under siege. Today, because of the season, all are being invited to sing Christmas carols before lunch. Some join in, many do not; the administrator of the place speaks in cajoling tones and is gently disregarded. The important work of this place is the stitching of gossip, present and past, into a quilt of history.

The noon siren blows, and the town's cafés begin to fill up. (Besides the Hiway 20, there are the Depot, Big John's, and, out by the East City Park, across from the empty swimming pool, the D & B.) Talk is of the coming Orange Bowl game and of the weather; a warm front is pushing its way northward, and it looks as if two low-pressure systems will link up over Colorado. The chance of snowfall has appeared in the forecast. Two factions have developed, those in favor and those against, and snow is being debated as if something could be done about it.

Downtown, at radio station KBRB, the announcer reads the news off the wire-service machine. He proceeds like a man slick-shod, crossing a frozen parking lot in a high wind; he pauses frequently to reassure himself with pat phrases, such as "items of news and information." He multiplies each category by two, so that there are "questions and queries," "happenings and events," "bulletins and announcements;" he sometimes skips names like Sihanouk and Khadafy, and is happiest reading sports scores.

Twenty miles away, our writer friend has just turned on the radio. When he hears, "That's all our news notes for today, back in a few seconds to give you some idea and indication on the weather situation shaping up for us here in the nation's midsection," he pushes up his eyeglasses with his middle finger and makes a dour face. "Nose newts," he mutters; he snaps the radio off without waiting for the forecast, rinses out a pan from the sink, and applies the opener to a can of split-pea soup. Busying himself at the kitchen counter, he bends to look skyward through the window. "Nice out," he says to himself; he frowns at the cattle rubbing against his fence. He stirs the soup, which is bubbling at the edges, and begins to think about the rest of his day. All he needs to do is cable half a stack of hay onto the haysled and scatter it, and string out a sack of cake behind the pickup. It shouldn't take longer than a couple of hours on a good warm day with no snow on the ground. If a storm does come, this much could be more than he can do.

By the time my father has gotten home from the Senior Citizens', kicked back in his recliner, turned on the Cable News Network and settled in for his third nap of the day, our imaginary writer and rancher (I don't really know anyone who's *that* crabby) has finished his soup and a can of peaches, put on his coveralls, boots, gloves, and stocking cap and is out the door. The yellow-and-white dog greets him with a fandango of pleasure, running outward in fast tight circles and returning shyly for a touch on the head. This is a proud dog who hardly ever barks, part border collie, with the quickness and some of the habits of a coyote; he hasn't forgotten that once he belonged only to himself, living on what he could steal. He considers the absent-minded man to whom he lowers his head a friend and an employer. The meals are bland but regular; he likes the work, outrunning and outwitting cattle, but he's always free to leave.

The Farmall "MD" our writer feeds with was built in 1949, which makes it a white-haired piece of machinery. It's a diesel that starts on gasoline, and it's a match for its driver when it comes to crankiness. He busies himself checking its vital fluids: antifreeze, crankcase oil, the oil in the reservoir of the injector pump, the fuel in the diesel tank, and the amount of gas in the small auxiliary tank that runs the engine while it's warming up. Every little thing is as it ought to be, so he disconnects the cord from the engine heater and climbs aboard. He opens the valve on the gasoline tank, pulls the choke out just so, checks the position of the gas/diesel crossover lever, and tramps the starter button with his heel. The starter grumps a couple of times, and the engine begins to putter quietly, barely alive. Now he fiddles the choke delicately in and out, watches the stack puff smoke, and listens anxiously for any hesitation. Slowly the old dinosaur gathers speed. Once it's humming nicely, he grasps the throttle in one hand and the crossover lever in the other. When he thrusts the crossover forward and jerks the throttle clockwise, the engine clatters as if someone were dribbling a handful of gravel through the intake manifold, and a thick gout of black and gray smoke rises from the stack.

Now the outdoor air penetrating his coveralls causes him to look around and sniff the breeze. He notes the attenuated sun, the hint of mist that thickens and chills the air, and he sees that the cattle are unusually restless and hungry.

"Storm coming. Isn't that right, Dobbie?"

Aaanhh! That *right*, Kemo Sabe, the dog thinks. Like the cattle, he's known about it for hours.

Our writer backs the tractor up to the haysled, and then the two of them take it across a wide cattle guard, down the road a quarter-mile, and through the gate to the stackyard. The dog darts in front of the cows that run behind, popping his teeth in their faces until the man can get the wire gate closed. Now, using a pitchfork, the man cleans loose hay away from one side of a stack; he pulls the haysled alongside, and removes the pin that couples the sled to the tractor. (It's not really a "sled," by the way, but a wooden platform balanced across two I-beams that are slung between truck axles.) A half-inch steel cable is pinned to the rear axle of the haysled. The man unhooks this cable and drags it around behind the stack to the front of the sled, where he drops it over a hook welded to the frame. Next he gets a tall "handy-man" jack and raises one side of the platform. He goes around the stack with the pitchfork, pulling loose hay up and kicking the cable under it; when he reaches the rear of the sled, he lifts the cable over the wheels and lays it across the frame, ready to hook on.

During the stack-loading operation that follows, our author abandons his morning's abstractions to give his mind over to a watchful attention to particulars; a winch is involved, winding the cable with several tons of force. At the coffee shop, he's seen the older men's hands, several of them missing the end joints of one or two fingers. Once the stackyard gate is closed, the dog runs up onto the moving haystack to ride high above the meadow and the herd; his pose is kingly and cheerful, for this is his hour of usefulness.

Now the routine business of feeding cattle will go forward. Taking his weather forecast from the animals, the man scatters the hay close to the windbreak, leaving enough on the sled for tomorrow's feeding. The hot blood singing in his cheeks rouses his sluggish spirit, and he forgets, for a couple of hours, to be un-happy.

About the time our writer is caking his cows—he turns his truck loose on the frozen meadow, idling in super-low, and jumps from the driver's seat to run and sit on the tailgate and dribble out the wafers from two fifty-pound paper sacks—the Hiway 20 Cafe is filling up once more with coffee drinkers. Because it's Friday, some of them have been gambling over at the Elks Club.

Scene: A public restaurant. Two rows of booths, with an elbow-high partition. In one booth an EIGHTY-YEAR-OLD MAN sits across from a YOUNGER MAN who will serve as audience. *Enter* FIRST CARD PLAYER, stage right; he stops at the adjoining booth.

1ST C.P.: (to older man) Anybody sittin' here?

80: No, and I'd just as soon keep it that way.

1ST C.P.: (to young man) 'S he been like this all day? (sits; to 80) By God, I'm sittin' down; if you don't like it, *you* can leave.

80: Well I *don't* like it, and I believe I can whip ya.

1ST C.P.: (starts to rise) All right! Out in the parking lot!

80: You go on out there and get to swingin'. I'll be right out as soon as I finish my coffee.

YOUNGER MAN: (to 1ST C.P.) You'd better watch out.

Last two fellas that went out there with him haven't been back.

1ST C.P.: He's the one should watch out. (to waitress) Gimme a hot tea. An' I wish the management'd do a better job of keepin' some of these bums out of here.

80: (to waitress) You'd better make sure he can pay. He looks down at the heels if you ask me.

1ST C.P.: Speak when you're spoken to, damn ya!

Enter SECOND CARD PLAYER: (mournfully) Anybody know where a fella could get a loan?

1ST C.P.: (laughs) A loan! You're the one's been rakin' in all the money!

2ND C.P.: (continues) Maybe a job sweepin' floors? Anything at all to get me through till payday.

80: Looks like today *is* payday, for the sharks.

2ND C.P.: (laughs) I think the sharks've all washed up on the beach.

1ST C.P.: (looks up) Hell, I seen you tuckin' away them twenties.

2ND C.P.: Ten dollars. That's all I made so far.

1ST C.P.: Me too. I figure I made about ten dollars.

2ND C.P.: (to 80) It's been a wonderful card game. Ev-erybody that's in it's ahead ten dollars. (to 1ST C.P.) Is it safe to sit here?

1ST C.P.: If you don't mind puttin' up with *him*.

2ND C.P.: (looks at 80; to 1ST C.P.) It ought to be all right. I see there's a partition between the two of ya. (sits; lowers voice) Say, you shouldn't've sent poor

Finney home cryin' the way you did with those three queens.

1ST C.P.: (laughs) By God, if it hadn't've been for them queens, *I'd* have gone home. You'd have to find someone else to buy your coffee.

2ND C.P.: Oh. Buyin' my coffee, are you? (to waitress) Guess I'll have that cup of coffee after all.

1ST C.P.: I didn't say that!

2ND C.P.: (to 80) Didn't he say he was buyin' me a cup of coffee?

1ST C.P.: (to 80) You keep out of this!

80: (to 2ND C.P.) The only thing I heard sounded like a pigeon cooin' out its last few dyin' breaths.

1ST C.P.: The only pigeons around here are the ones flyin' in and out of your head.

80: I'd rather have pigeons than bats in my belfry. (to 2ND C.P.) You should be ashamed to take money from the mentally incompetent.

1ST C.P.: (to 2ND C.P.) Pay no attention to him. He's got that Old-Timer's Disease.

2ND C.P.: (to 80) Did you say incompetent? Or incontinent? (laughter. This talk, like the poker game at the Elks, could go on all weekend. Any losers will be soothed and tended; the real winners will be those lucky enough to have sat in for free.)

The few women who coffee at the Hiway 20 smoke a lot of cigarettes. They sit together at one of the booths; their laughter carries tobacco smoke upward to mingle with the men's. Lots of cancer in this country, high blood pressure, heart trouble. Who knows about sex? These midafternoon loiterers are middle-aged and older. People marry early and go to work, then develop an appetite for gossip and see-through coffee after forty. Young men will tell you there aren't enough single women around; the women say, not enough single men. Both would like more variety, nothing new for a small town.

Our writer, a single man, finishes his feeding by five o'clock, leaving plenty of time for him to clean up and make the drive to Ainsworth. It's Friday night, the beginning of the Christmas holidays, and there'll be fresh faces at the Frontier. The overcast has thickened toward sunset but there's no snow yet; he could go in just for an hour or two, keep an eye toward the window and bolt for home if the weather changes.

On the other hand . . . His fresh-air mood doesn't last five minutes once he's in the door. He keeps the house too hot, and it makes him feel lethargic. Friday night is know-it-all night on Nebraska Public Television; "Washington Week in Review" and "Wall Street Week" are two programs he doesn't like to miss. If he drives to town it'll cost him two gallons of gas each way, plus a meal, plus whatever he spends for drinks at the Frontier. And the odds are they won't play the kind of music—R & B, sixties and seventies rock—he likes to dance to.

He makes up his mind to take a shower, at least. The shower's in a rusty, rectangular enameled-tin box full of mold and spiders, fed by a pump that has a habit of quitting in the middle of things. Sure enough, just when he's wet down and halfway covered with soap, the water drizzles away to a cold trickle; he has to run shivering onto the porch, grab a hammer, open the cellar door, and go down and bang on the housing until the pump starts. Dressing, he discovers that all his newer shirts are in the dirty-clothes pile; when he turns on the TV to catch "The McNeil-Lehrer Report," he sees in the upper right-hand corner of the screen the NPTV weather symbol, a stylized W inside a circle.

"Monkey nuts," he growls. A fluey ache has settled in his joints. He puts some potatoes on to boil; he's staying home.

In Ainsworth, sometime after seven o'clock, a transformation takes place in the sleepy streets. Pickup trucks with blue or amber running-board lights, compact cars a few years old, and several repainted tuned-up Mustangs and Firebirds and Camaros begin a noisy L-shaped parade, from a U-turn at the south end of Main Street north to Highway 20, east through town to another U-turn at the entrance to the East City Park, and back again. A few of them pull off to clog the apron at Masters', the gas station and convenience store that forms the other half of the Hiway 20 Cafe complex. These are Brown County's mysterious teen-agers,

joined tonight by a few returning college students. Knots of belligerent-looking boys cluster just outside the entrance, their loud, self-consciously obscene insult-greetings sending wisps of vapor into the air; blonde, frizzy-headed, thin-hipped girls come and go. No adult knows what they say to each other. Inside the building are stacks and rows of six-packs of wine coolers and beer, legally beyond the reach of eighteen-year-olds. Through some psychokinetic process based on fervent desire, by midnight a certain amount of these liquids will be miraculously transferred through the walls and into the cabs of the waiting pickups.

Across the street and a half-block east, more cars and pickup trucks are gathering. Of the town's five bars, only the Frontier has live music on a regular basis; tonight Bill Legate, a local favorite, has come round on the circuit. The music will be country-western, with a sprinkling of Cajun and bouncy seventies rock: "Left a good job in the city, workin' for the man every night an' day. . . ." The crowd shaping up is a good mix of town and ranch people of different ages, though the younger folk predominate. The Front takes up most of a large steel building that also contains a laundromat and Junior Weander's used-car-dealing office; the interior is paneled with slate-gray fiberglass "stone" masonry. It has everything it needs, pool tables in the back room, a sizable dance floor, a juke box and a color TV, and a good long bar with mirrors. Weeknights with no band in town it tends to seem gloomy and cavernous, but tonight it will be packed and jumping.

The other bars in town are also doing good business. On Main Street, the Longhorn is where it's always been, across from the Coast-to-Coast store and the bank. (That's not quite how it ought to be put, because the Longhorn has been there longer than either of them; some of the customers look like they've been there that long as well.) Down at the other end of Main, the Silver Circle shares a new brick building with a saddle shop. On the highway, the Golden Steer is a short walk for those who get crowded out at the Front, and further out, east of town, the lounge at the bowling alley serves drinks long after the last pin clatters to the boards.

There's a lot of traffic tonight, a lot of circulation among these places, none of it on foot or horseback. The Brown County Sheriff's Department makes the best of it, keeping a patrol car visible along the highway. The folks in from farms and ranches can't be expected to walk home, and on the other hand it just wouldn't seem fair to ask them all to stay sober.

Meanwhile, south of Long Pine, the Lone Ranger is staying sober. Tired of television, tired of literature, tired of *Playboy* and its unattainables, he thumbs through a stack of well-worn *National Geographic*s. He considers the writing to bear the same relationship to English prose as elevator music has to Creedence Clearwater Revival, but some few of the photographs fascinate him: a twelve-year-old woman-child from India, big angry eyes toward the camera, her young brother lugged on one bony hip; the strobe-lit face of a leopard seal, shot by reflex in underwater desperation as the photographer reacted to a shape looming under the ice; another seal, this one no more than a dot high above a lagoon (photo taken from an airplane) with a fountain of spray below, where a killer whale has used its flukes to toss the four-hundred-pound animal like a cat batting a mouse.

The issue he chooses tonight examines the lost civilization of the Incas. It contains a photo of one of the streets of Macchu Picchu, with a curved wall of fitted stones rising toward a flat-topped pyramid, nothing but bald sky and bare stone in the background. He re-reads paragraphs he has read a dozen times; by the yellow lamp, as the night deepens, he nods above the photograph, and the curved wall becomes an exit ramp, the pyramid a line of skyscrapers in the distance . . .

Outside, somewhere beyond the stackyard, a coyote yips. The dog lying beneath the lighted window lifts his head, ears alert, then sighs and rests his muzzle on his paws. Something white and tiny as a star drifts silently across the lamplight to nestle in the brittle grass; at eleven minutes past midnight, the first flake falls.

The Virtues of Abandonment

It's October, 1991: a different year, another country. I've moved to Lincoln, become a shuffler among bricky hallways, scattering the gray dandruff of wisdom out over the shining heads of the young. It's a lot of fun, some weeks; other times it seems a good way to get old fast. Instead of years, I think semesters, and grade papers one set at a time.

Today, though . . . Today is one of those priceless autumn days when the sky's as blue as your grade-school sweetheart's eyes. My car's blue too, blue like an old pair of navy socks; a gasping ten-year-old Granada, a teacher's car, not above middling reliable. But it's a car, and I like cars, and today I'm driving up from Lincoln to Ainsworth. A high privilege to be dodging work on such a day.

I get breakfast eaten and my teeth brushed and my crippled old dog loaded in the back seat, and I'm out on the street by a quarter after nine. I still have to get gas and stop by the campus to check my mail, so it's ten-thirty by the time I turn onto O Street, headed west. All morning I have passed by and driven beneath golden ash and rusty elm, have been dazzled by purple crabapple and ornamental pear, have seen sun-blown maples flashing every maple color. Even Lincoln's anemic pin oaks are caught up in the blaze, those that've had their iron shots a downright bloody red. Next to

Morrill Hall a tamarack is trying to achieve the hue Titian's redheads are noted for, a darkening and glorification of bronze. A city in Technicolor, green to yellow to red to purple to brown; and why leave town?

Well, there are business reasons, and there are personal reasons. Lincoln, to be plain, gets on my nerves. Too many cars, too many bricks, too much money in the styrofoam-desert downtown. Too many pretty women on campus, all too young for me, but my eyes too often think they have to follow one. Too-solid unanimity in the football Saturday that's coming. Too much happening that doesn't really concern me; I'm headed home to reset my small-town clock. I'll pass through a piece of the sandhills on the way.

West O Street is torn up, as usual. Past the barricades I catch the ramp that leads to Interstate 80, and take my first breath of highway air. No shortage of oxygen in October; still, I heave a sigh at the city limits. I settle in for the cruise to Grand Island, and watch the corn and soybean and milo fields go past. This end of Nebraska's still very much the Midwest; the loess hills roll away like Iowa, russet, yellow, brown. The brambles in the gullies would do as well in Ohio. Fall color bathes the corners of my vision, but while I'm on the Interstate I don't see much. I've driven this stretch a hundred times, maybe more, and repetition has made me stupid; I spend the first ninety minutes waiting for the trip to start.

I-80 is notorious for following the Platte, flat as water itself, but this far east the Platte loops north toward Columbus. If the sailor Columbus had gotten this far, he would've found recognizable towns, the earth lodges of the Pawnee, who grew corn and squash on these same hills until Oregon Trail times. In a real sense, I-80 *is* the Oregon Trail, horsepower replacing bull power while the petroleum lasts; its famous flatness is like the intermontane flatness of the West. The traveler on the Platte River road is driving up an easy grade built by water carrying bits of the Rocky Mountains, ground to sand.

Farther west, the Platte forms the southern boundary of the sandhills. Does the river stop the hills' migration by washing away their sandy toes? Or did the ancestral Platte beget the dunes, bringing sand from the mountains to be left high and dry on sandbars, then whisked northward by the parching *foehns* that rake the plains in summer? Nebraska sandhills sand is finer-textured and rounder than Cape Cod beach sand. Maybe that means it's older; in the earth's vast geological seasons, sand gets recycled, buried and compressed to sandstone and then exhumed by wind and water and worn away to sand again. A grain could've been rounded in the sea a hundred million years ago, then locked in sandstone until last week. Would it then be older or younger than its angular brother, chipped from granite by a glacier and sloshing around out there on the coast since the latest ice age? It's a question for geologists and John McPhee.

When I see the Aurora exit I start to come out of my trance. I used to stop in Aurora for lunch sometimes; there's a good roast-beef sort of café along the old highway. My mother's mother's family landed in Nebraska somewhere south of here, not your taciturn Swedes but a merry bunch with a streak of music and a taste for wandering. Great-grandpa Johnson, it is said, did not object to being paid for his fiddling in whiskey. He arrived in New York City by jumping ship from the Swedish navy, and died somewhere in California on his way to the Alaska gold rush.

I used to avoid Grand Island by taking the second exit north to Highway 2, but more commonly now I use the first exit, then take a complicated route that skirts the east edge of town, passing near the airport. This puts me on Highway 281, heading north toward St. Paul and, if I would persist, O'Neill. At St. Paul I take a bit of Highway 92 to the west, then turn north on 11 toward Ord and Burwell, then west on 91 to Taylor. What these bits and pieces amount to is a route that follows the North Loup River; if I want, I can stay with it all the way to Brewster, directly south of Ainsworth on Highway 7.

These Loup Valley towns are like my home town in size and in a few more intangible measures—ratio of pickup trucks to Volvos, height of water tower, number of calories per serving of pie. The economies are similar: irrigated corn, soybeans, a little alfalfa in the valley;

clay hills to the south, and north of the river the sand-hills, provide grazing for cattle. Their "Class B" high schools annually send kids to Lincoln to the state basketball and volleyball tournaments, to be whipped by teams from the populated end of the state, York or Wahoo or Lincoln Pius X. Social Security is a mainstay of the economy, as is an upstream dam providing water for gravity irrigation. Hunting and fishing bring in a few tourist dollars, but most tourists are people who grew up in the area, coming back to give their offspring a look. There's a small, dispersed manufacturing industry producing items useful in agriculture: corral panels, round bale feeders, irrigation equipment. Ford dealer, Chevy dealer, John Deere dealer, banker, lawyer, undertaker are the substantial men of town; an occasional farmer or rancher arrives at millionaire status, but the majority are lucky to stay afloat. In general these are stable communities, poor rather than wealthy but without much poverty in the ghetto or Appalachian sense. I customarily make two stops along this route: one in St. Paul for gasoline (cheaper than it'll be in Ainsworth) and one at a little rest area along Highway 11, near Scotia.

To my disgust, I find that the rest area has been vandalized. A handsome aluminum sign giving the history of the chalk mine that once operated here has been knocked off its pillars, and the concrete pillars themselves have been broken. It must've taken a four-wheel-drive truck with a heavy bumper to do this; as I look at it I have a sinking feeling that it won't be repaired. When I try the old-fashioned pump to get some water for my dog, I find the pump-rod is broken also, and I fear for the pump itself, valuable in some circles as an antique.

This little stopping-place has been a pivot for many pleasant trips, winter, spring, summer, and fall. I feel angry and sad that the destroyers have found it out and laid rough hands on its quietness. I help my old dog out of the car, and we go for a walk here as is our custom, but even as I turn my back on the broken sign and follow the short trail up the canyon, I seem to hear drunken shouts and the snarl of an outsized engine, the shattering of a bottle and the concrete breaking.

What belongs to the public belongs to no one, and whatever lies abandoned can be trashed. That is the argument I hear in the crunch of gravel, in the rustle of fallen leaves around my feet. At the end of the path I hear a turkey gobble. The sun's behind the hill, the blue day cooling. My dog has her nose in the leaves.

Back on the highway, I'm haunted by a sudden nostalgia. I think of the friend who first showed me the chalk mine, a gentle microbiologist who fell in love with wood. He turned carpenter, lives in Phoenix now, where he's become a builder of houses. One more good man gone from the country.

This far north and west of Lincoln, October's been

more persuasive with the trees; in particular, the ashes' golden fivefold leaves have fallen. In the planted windbreaks, Chinese elms are still green, but along the river the brush has the purple-gray color of bare stems and branches.

Across the river to the north, for some time now, there have been the shapes of hills. Here on the south side, where the highway is, the hills are clay, and the clay hills run north from St. Paul about as far as Greeley; but the hills over the river have a sandhill look about them, the way the rounded tops continue off like waves to the horizon.

My jubilation at having ditched my responsibilities in Lincoln has passed. Though the sky remains blue, I feel as though I've driven under the leading edge of a cold front. Doubts like buzzards ride the shoulder of the wind. I'm driving the road I took to college, a third of a normal lifetime ago; and with what news am I returning? That the roadside pulloff by Scotia's been marred by thugs? I decide to stop in Taylor for a piece of pie.

Taylor is a little town full of big cottonwoods, built on Loup River sand. Its most notable feature is a block-square park, around which the one-story businesses sit. The only building worth looking at is abandoned to storage; it's an old mansard-roofed hotel and grocery that sits across the highway from the square's northeast corner. The trees in the park are immense and broadly spaced, and all around their leaves lie glittering in the sun like metal, like leaves from a tree of brass.

The café's in a green stucco building a block west of the intersection, one of those places where the locals know to serve themselves but the waitress will come over if you look like a stranger. I guess I look strange enough, because she brings the pot over and offers me coffee. I say no thanks, what kind of pie have you got, and she looks toward the counter as if to say, see for yourself. I get chocolate pie with the meringue wilted back from the tip, nice and sticky on top where it's dried out a bit. It's the coffee hour, and several men share a long table in the center of the café. They're older mostly, overweight mostly, some of them looking crippled up, more like farmers than ranchers though there's not a great distinction in this country. They look me over and go on smoking and talking. The room is dark, more like a bar than a café, but the pie is good and the silverware's clean.

The chocolate goes to work, cheering me up, and I'm thinking I should give myself a break. What did he want, that boy who passed through here in his hand-me-down Ford, all those years ago? I thought I'd like to be an engineer; the uncle I was named after was a builder of dams, and I thought his an admirable life. Today I'd vote to leave most rivers undisturbed. I thought I'd work for the government, a safe job with a fat salary, and since last year I do work for the university part-time, and make enough to feed my dog canned food three times a week. If I'd become that engineer, would I feel better at forty-five? Or would I wish I'd had the time to sit and write poetry?

I could go west toward Brewster, or north toward Bassett. Because the sun is slanting toward the horizon, I choose north. The shadow of my car will zoom close and dart away again as I pass the hills and hollows along the grade; it's a friendly sort of rubber-band attachment, that dark and weightless clown-car that bounces at the edge of vision: memento mori, butterfly of death. This stretch of 183 is sandhills all the way, with the hamlet of Rose the only town in sixty miles. Do-it-yourself Interstate, a great road if you're in a hurry.

Now I am in the kingdom of grass: not a landscape without trees, but one in which each tree is noteworthy.

This set of essays was supposed to be about the sandhills. I find myself in the middle of them, with nothing to say. Here are the grasses in their fall colors, yellow to purplish-pink, passing through a thousand shades of salmon; here are the hills themselves, their thousand hollows with no outlet for rainwater other than up or down. Here's the water, come out from a sidehill to form a pond, a few late ducks among the cattails. Here is sand, visible from time to time in the shoulder of the road or in blowouts, or in cowpaths cut into the thin skin of buffalo grass. Here are barbed-wire fences, an occasional grove and set of buildings, a mailbox.

I have tried to tell the truth, and I'm afraid I've tried harder not to; I've spoken ill of the living and of the dead. The last time I saw Joe Carlsen, the hired man who taught us to use the Farmhand stacker, who renamed Dad's favorite horse, who kept the house shipshape by hiding his dirty dishes under the sink, he was sitting on cold concrete, his back against a filling station across the alley from the Silver Circle, legs out in a flat V, belly over legs, hat slumped over belly. Anyone could see the booze had used him up, that he was sitting there watching the hours fall, waiting to die. Fifteen years ago. I remember it clearly, because I passed by as if I did not know the man.

Here's a narrow highway, here's a dot, a speeding car, here's a man passing through. If I were a photographer, I'd shoot this from a satellite, just as I crossed the horizon moving west, just as the continent turned her green-furred back to the light. Just before I caught up with the sun on my way to China.

Other volumes in the
Great Plains Photography
Series include:

Dreams in Dry Places
By Roger Bruhn

*Eyewitness at Wounded
Knee* By Richard E.
Jensen, R. Eli Paul,
and John E. Carter

*A Harmony of the Arts:
The Nebraska State Capitol*
Edited by Frederick C.
Luebke

Designed by Dika Eckersley
Typeset by Keystone Typesetting,
Inc., in Adobe Minion designed
by Robert Slimbach.